"Want to learn how to become a ᵍ_____ ___ ᵢₙₛₚᵢᵣₑ your people? This book teaches you the secrets of how your body language can elevate your ability to lead and achieve extraordinary results!"

—CHESTER ELTON,
cofounder of The Culture Works, author of multiple award-winning
#1 *New York Times*, *USA Today*, and *Wall Street Journal* bestsellers,
including *All In*, *The Carrot Principle*, and *Leading with Gratitude*

"A remarkable book packed full of insights and tools that turn managers into leaders and leaders into team-leading titans. Using her vast knowledge and experience, Kasia Wezowski weaves communication skills, body language, and emotional intelligence into a superpower formula that puts integrity and authenticity at the forefront of cutting-edge business." **—PETER SAGE,**
founder of Sage Academy,
international bestselling author of *The Inside Track*

"*Language That Leads* is a sacred exploration of leadership through the lens of movement, communication behaviors, and expressions. As a former dancer and choreographer, Kasia developed the BLINK method that offers an analysis of micro expressions and body language and their relationship to leadership, shining a light on how our physicality and expressions can influence our teams, our communities, and our families. Kasia lovingly and personally guides the reader by sharing tactical examples and also vulnerable truths in service of the reader's desire to become an enlightened leader." **—TRICIA BROUK,**
award-winning director, producer, author,
and founder of The Big Talk Academy

"Kasia describes ten important skills of a leader that help to bring leaders to the next level of communication. Based on authentic, empathetic interaction between leaders and their teams, this book shows a new approach to leadership." **—GARRY RIDGE,**
the Culture Coach,
chairman emeritus of WD-40 Company

"Kasia Wezowski's new masterpiece *Language That Leads* brings to life how you can become the kind of leader who can harness the human factor to realize your potential and performance and that of your team and organization." —JAMES M. CITRIN,

"Kasia's book is written from a unique slant. First, as a documentary filmmaker, she's studied leadership through the lens of a camera. That angle gives her an acute focus. Second, her deep expertise in body language positions her to explain how leadership is very behavioral, how so much of it is a visible, physical act. In human interactions, the body always speaks first! Scans by fMRI machines show that our brain's mirror neurons fire off in the first 1/20 of a second of a social encounter, faster than you can even think, instantly influencing how the other person responds. Your body language needs to be preset—already in place—so you project effectively and shape the behavior of others appropriately. Also, Kasia's BLINK technique provides a snazzy two-minute drill for reading a person's micro expressions and managing the interaction. This is a great tactical manual on how to lead." —PRICE PRITCHETT, PHD,

"Kasia Wezowski's *Language That Leads* avoids the bane of many leadership books—too many ideas and not enough practical solutions—and rewards the reader with pragmatic strategies to actually lead better. Wezowski focuses on leader communication, the delivery of the leader's influence, and does it in a way that encourages application and practice. Read *Language That Leads* to make yourself a better leader. Kasia Wezowski is a prolific author, and each of her books has been better than the last, with *Language That Leads* standing as a masterpiece. I could not put down this book." —TOM KOLDITZ, PHD,

"A must-have book for leaders who would like to design the communication they love with authenticity." —AYSE BIRSEL,

LANGUAGE THAT LEADS

Communication Strategies
That **Inspire** and **Engage**

KASIA WEZOWSKI

WITH A FOREWORD BY MARSHALL GOLDSMITH

HarperCollins
LEADERSHIP

An Imprint of HarperCollins

Published by HarperCollins Leadership, an imprint of HarperCollins Focus LLC.

Any internet addresses, phone numbers, or company or product information printed in this book are offered as a resource and are not intended in any way to be or to imply an endorsement by HarperCollins Leadership, nor does HarperCollins Leadership vouch for the existence, content, or services of these sites, phone numbers, companies, or products beyond the life of this book.

Book design by Aubrey Khan, Neuwirth & Associates, Inc.

ISBN 978-1-4002-3660-2 (eBook)
ISBN 978-1-4002-3659-6 (TP)

Library of Congress Control Number: 2023931456

Printed in the United States of America
23 24 25 26 27 LBC 5 4 3 2 1

CONTENTS

PART 1

OUTER SKILLS

PART 2

INNER SKILLS

CONTENTS

PART 3
GROWTH SKILLS

FOREWORD

A leader's communication has ripple effects throughout an entire organization and can be the deciding factor between the success or failure of even the largest companies.

No matter our jobs, we all face situations in life and work when we are called upon to lead. And when those moments happen, our communication style becomes more critical than ever. I believe every effective leader needs to learn fluency in the language of leadership.

Leaders who speak this language not only have a positive impact on others, they also elevate the way everyone in their organization communicates with one another, resulting in better understanding, less resentment, and drastically improved results.

My friend Alan Mulally understood this. Alan took over as the CEO of Ford Motor Company in 2006 at a time when the company was losing billions and the stock price was plummeting. Alan's turnaround of the company is regarded as one of the great corporate success stories of our time. And it began with communication.

Alan deployed a "no defects" approach to communication, insisting on politeness and treating others with respect and consideration at all times, with no exceptions. If a cell phone was used during a meeting, the meeting was stopped. If someone made a sarcastic remark, that behavior was quickly corrected. The intervention began at the top, and Alan ensured it was witnessed by people at the company at all levels. By modeling considerate communication, the entire corporate culture changed, and success followed in its wake.

Leaders need to be especially sensitive to their communication because their position of authority means that even the smallest verbal or nonverbal cues can have enormous impact on their staff. For example, I often caution leaders against using the word *but* because this three-letter, one-syllable word can have a disproportionately destructive impact on the results of your communication.

When the word *but* follows positive feedback, it tends to erase the emotional impact of whatever came before it. If you tell someone, "You approached this project with care, insight, and diligence, *but* the finer details need some more refining," all that the person will actually hear is, "The finer details need more refining." Imagine that whatever you said *after* the word "but" is the only thing the person hears, and you'll understand the true impact you are having.

This example highlights the difference between good communication and poor communication. When you are communicating well, what you *say* is the same as what someone *hears*. And when you are listening well, what you *hear* is the same as what the other person is *saying*.

Today, more and more leaders are also called upon to manage "knowledge workers." These are professionals and subject matter experts who know more about their particular field of expertise than the people managing them do. *Telling* things to these people is not enough. To be an effective leader, you also need to be able to *ask* and be able to *learn*.

Peter Drucker is the founder of modern management and was my mentor for many years. Peter had a knack for knowing where management was heading long before most managers figured it out. When Peter said, "The leader of the past was a person who knew how to *tell*. The leader of the future will be a person who knows how to *ask*," he was referring to an idea that forms the core of Kasia Wezowski's book *Language That Leads*.

Communication as a leader in today's world has three phases:

1. Asking for input
2. Understanding input
3. Responding to input

I can summarize this formula in four words: Ask. Listen. Think. Thank. To be successful at this, you need to be able to accept what others are saying to you from a place of genuine openness and curiosity. This means getting beyond your ego and exercising a certain level of self-control. As Frances Hesselbein, the longtime CEO of the Girl Scouts of America, says, "How can you be expected to control others if you can't control yourself?"

As Kasia explores in this book, great communication is not simply something you do; it's not just a few behaviors that can be memorized and imitated. It's also a deeper level of understanding of yourself and the careful cultivation of qualities that will help you earn the right to lead and direct other people. Leadership is a way of being, and it is also, as this book explores, a holistic language.

When you understand the language of leadership, both when *listening* and when *speaking*, you will be able to ensure that you are successful across the entire spectrum of your communication.

Whether you're a corporate executive, a start-up founder, a parent, spouse, or someone working your way toward the top, there are moments in your life when you are called upon to seize the mantle of leadership, whether for a moment or for years. And even outside of those special moments, the keys to communication that are explored in this book will help you shine and facilitate others to shine as well. The result will make you not only better at communicating to others but also better at receiving communication from others.

● ● ●

MARSHALL GOLDSMITH is the Thinkers50 #1 Executive Coach and *New York Times* bestselling author of *The Earned Life*, *Triggers*, and *What Got You Here Won't Get You There*.

INTRODUCTION

There's an internal struggle happening within every leader: A leader wants to be perfect. At the same time, perfection is impossible. It's not even always *desirable*. Perfection means that nothing can or should be changed. It refers to a permanent state. Leadership, however, is fluid. It is something that you need to live day by day. Leaders may be able to create perfect *systems*, but the human element will always introduce the need for change. Therefore, true perfection can never exist.

Leadership As a *Kasuri* Pattern

To understand how imperfection is actually the source of great leadership, I like to think about *kasuri* (絣), a type of Japanese fabric design and patterning. *Kasuri* is a fabric that has been woven with thread fibers carefully dyed to create interwoven patterns. The designs look splashed, blurry, imperfect. This smudged look is not an error. In fact, it is inherent to the beauty of the *kasuri* patterns.

Once, the royal family in Okinawa attempted to create a *kasuri* pattern that was perfect, with straight lines and perfectly aligned patterns. The result was a piece that was clean but could not be called *kasuri*. It lacked the beauty of the classic, smudged patterns, and so the quest for perfection was abandoned.

In *The Beauty of Everyday Things*, author Soetsu Yanagi explains how the imperfection of *kasuri*—its smudged effect—is not a flaw but rather its very essence: "Without this rubbing or smudging, *kasuri* could never have been. . . . It is precisely this misalignment and blurry effect that is the source of *kasuri*'s beauty."

Creating *kasuri* requires a special process under specific conditions. The process is carried about by humans, who will inevitably make some mistakes. But within the context of this process, mistakes and errors actually enhance the resulting beauty.

Leadership is, in many ways, the same. No system you create will be followed by perfect, identical robots. The human element will impose itself and make itself evident through small differences. How you manage these differences and master this subtle interplay of forces will determine your success as a leader.

According to *Inc.* magazine, most companies only operate at 30 percent of their potential. In *Language That Leads*, we will look at how you can become the kind of leader who can harness the human factor to raise the potential and performance of individuals and organizations.

Inspired by Marshall Goldsmith's people-centered leadership philosophy and informed by my own experience as a student of human nature through the study of micro expressions and body language, we will explore how you as a leader can place yourself in alignment with the people who make up the systems and organizations that you work with.

•

Leadership As Communication, Not Command

Leadership used to be synonymous with authority. Leaders would give orders, and others would follow. Not anymore. In today's dynamic business culture, leadership is about facilitation, not force, communication, command. Leaders of the future need to use their empathy and influence to bring out the potential of their employees and let each individual shine. To stay relevant in this new reality, leadership training is long overdue for an upgrade.

Language That Leads is a practical guide for growing into a leader of the future. Through clear advice and real-world examples, you will discover in these pages how changing the language you use and improving the way you communicate, not only with others but also with yourself, will result in greater engagement, efficacy, and impact across the board.

Each chapter in this book is based around a core quality of leadership, as identified by Marshall Goldsmith. We will explore each idea in practical detail, explaining how it can be expressed, observed, and projected through both verbal and nonverbal communication. From specific, powerful techniques to big picture principles, you will discover how to measurably increase your impact as a leader of organizations and people.

HERE'S A SNEAK PEAK OF WHAT YOU'RE ABOUT TO LEARN . . .

- New leadership—why leaders of the future need to be different from leaders of the past
- Micro expressions—how reading these brief flashes of facial expression is the key to understanding and interpreting the honest emotions of others
- The body language of leadership—what your posture, gestures, and stance say to others, and how to control this
- Feedforward, not feedback—Marshall Goldsmith's approach for how successful leaders communicate
- Emotional intelligence—how to effectively manage others as a facilitator, not a dictator
- Intuitive decision-making—how effective leaders trust their empathy and make decisions from the gut
- BLINK—my signature technique for interpreting someone's true feelings about a situation or idea in under two minutes by observing body language and micro expressions
- The leadership mindset—how to think and therefore act as a leader
- Values-driven leadership—how to lead with integrity by tuning in to the core values that drive individuals and businesses

The book is divided into three overarching segments: Outer Skills, which you display and perform; Inner Skills, which you embody; and Growth Skills, which will impel your holistic evolution as a leader and also as a person.

Each chapter will cover an essential leadership quality, such as adaptability or empathy. We'll explore how you can recognize this quality in others and display yourself congruently with the whole spectrum of your verbal and nonverbal communication. Each chapter will cover the following elements:

- Why this leadership quality is important
- How you can nurture this quality in yourself
- How you can observe this quality in others
- How you can make your body language congruent with that quality
- How to recognize this quality using the BLINK technique

Having been inspired by Marshall Goldsmith throughout my career, it is an enormous pleasure and privilege to be able to introduce his wisdom to you here in these pages. Combined with my own experiences and expertise, the result is a journey into the heart of what it means to be a successful leader in today's world. I am so excited to be able to embark on this journey with you now.

KASIA WEZOWSKI
September 2022

PART 1

OUTER SKILLS

CHAPTER ONE

ADAPTABILITY

● ● ● ● ● ● ● ● ●

In *The Earned Life*, a film exploring the legacy of Marshall Goldsmith, Goldsmith stresses the idea that the job of a leader is not to be the smartest or most impressive person in the room; it's to get the best out of everybody in order to have the best team possible.

During the film, Goldsmith takes a moment to reflect on a simple Buddhist idea: *Every time I take a breath, it's a new me.* This is, in Goldsmith's view, true for each person. People are constantly changing, so each time you come to a meeting or introduce a new person to a team, you must be able to adapt in order to get the most out of each person's skill set.

Only when you are able to develop this kind of adaptability will you finally be able to create the best team possible.

WHY ADAPTABILITY IS AN IMPORTANT
LEADERSHIP QUALITY

Change is one constant that any business can count on. The worldwide pandemic of 2020 was only the latest reminder that adaptability is essential for a person or business hoping to ride out the daily, monthly, and yearly changes.

While the recent pandemic may feel like the biggest change businesses have faced, the last thirty years have actually seen businesses become less stable due to economic instability. The changes can't be stopped or delayed, which is why it's crucial to develop adaptability as a leader.

Adaptability may feel especially important when facing changing external circumstances, but it's about more than this. It's about adapting to people as well.

When you work as the leader of a team and are able to open yourself up to the emotions of those around you, you may observe that people are constantly experiencing changes within themselves, including changing emotional states. By learning to navigate those states, you can improve the quality of your team's work.

THE IMPORTANCE OF COMMUNICATION

Communication is what will allow you to get clarity from those around you, which will help you adapt to changing circumstances. Conveying what you want from people and how you want it done is essential.

Adaptability also involves welcoming communication from the other person, including how they feel about a task, how motivated they are to fulfill what is demanded of them, and what they would like to bring to the table. Being open to their ideas can help you know exactly what needs to be changed in order to get the most from their skill set.

Being a leader is no longer a one-way street. To be truly successful as a leader, you must build a two-way street that will allow people to come to you with ideas and feedback.

MANAGING SECRETS

In *The Earned Life*, Goldsmith speaks with Alan Mulally, former CEO of Ford, US CEO of the Year, and *Fortune*'s #3 World's Greatest Leaders. Mulally describes how he adapted to his team by creating a system he calls "managing secrets."

The system involves three colors: green, yellow, and red. If the members of his team showed a green board, it meant that they saw no problems and were good with the plan. Yellow meant they saw an issue and had a solution. Red meant they saw a problem but didn't have a solution.

Originally, people were reluctant to show anything but a green board, fearing backlash, but when one red board finally came up, Mulally responded by encouraging the team member to explore solutions to the problem he had identified. Within a week, a solution had been found.

The other employees then felt more comfortable using yellow and red because they finally felt empowered to identify problems and explore solutions once Mulally had responded positively to the first red board.

By adapting his system to encourage all team members to participate, Mulally was able to guide Ford through an impending crisis and recover using the strengths of each employee.

This shows why it's important to not only give instructions and assume that things will go well but to listen to the team and make sure you're getting the most out of each person by playing to their strengths and knowledge. Being open to this kind of reality check can be the difference between success and failure.

ADAPTABILITY AVOIDS STRESS CAUSED BY CHANGES

Change can cause stress, and leaders need to be prepared to use adaptability to help their team avoid this.

When you don't know how to announce or communicate changes, it can wreak havoc. People won't be able to understand or follow the changes, making it impossible for them to comply. At that point, the brain develops a state of high frequency beta waves due to stress, which are distracting and inhibit focus and creativity, two crucial elements needed when a company is facing any change.

To avoid this, leaders should manage the speed at which they present changes. Adapting to what your team can handle and providing them with enough details, instructions, and learning tools along the way can eliminate high levels of stress and encourage the creativity a company needs.

Developing Adaptability

Adaptability is a key quality for those who want to be successful. But how can you recognize this quality in yourself, or in others?

Imagine the following scenario. Each day, you go to work by car using the same route. On the way, you listen to a morning radio show, stop to have a coffee at a small coffee shop, and do your best to relax, arriving five minutes before you're due to be at work. One day, you find that a stretch of the highway you always use has been shut down, so you're unable to take the route you always drive and visit the little coffee shop that's on the way.

How do you react? The autopilot that usually takes over the second you slide into your car shuts down, and you are confronted with an unfamiliar situation. Do you panic, get angry, feel frustrated, or swear a lot? Do you take a deep breath, get creative, and pull out your phone to find another route with a coffee shop on the way? Are you able to maintain some mental balance, even when you pull into work five minutes late?

To get an idea of how adaptable you are, I invite you to write down the various emotions you imagine you could feel when faced with the situation described. Rate each emotion on a scale of 1–10. Do the negative or positive emotions and reactions get a higher score?

With this kind of scaling system, you can measure your ability to adapt to change. If the positive emotions and reactions scored higher, you will likely stay calm when faced with something unexpected and will be more likely to use creativity to find a solution. If the negative emotions and reactions scored higher, indicating low adaptability skills, you are more likely to suffer when something is out of place, forcing you to move out of auto-pilot and leaving a sense of resentment during the day ahead.

If you find that you have room for improvement when it comes to adaptability, all is not lost. Adaptability is, fortunately, a skill you can practice.

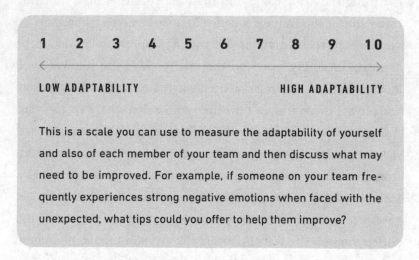

| 1 | 2 | 3 | 4 | 5 | 6 | 7 | 8 | 9 | 10 |

LOW ADAPTABILITY   HIGH ADAPTABILITY

This is a scale you can use to measure the adaptability of yourself and also of each member of your team and then discuss what may need to be improved. For example, if someone on your team frequently experiences strong negative emotions when faced with the unexpected, what tips could you offer to help them improve?

PRACTICING ADAPTABILITY

Adaptability is easy to develop when you dedicate yourself to making small changes to your routine each day. With these small changes, your brain will learn to expect the unexpected, so that when a more serious change or shift arises, you are more prepared.

For example, you can consciously decide to take a different route to work one or two days a week. If you're a leader, you can decide to have a meeting with employees in a different setting; if you always meet in the same room, perhaps gather everyone outside on a nice day.

The more creative and courageous you become with the changes you make in your life, the more adaptable you become.

When you begin to practice adaptability, you prepare yourself for new circumstances and train yourself to keep your options open. As I mentioned, change is a constant every person and business can count on. And this is a good thing, as it's only through change that progress can be made. When we develop adaptability and consciously choose to make changes instead of letting them surprise us at every turn, progress becomes the norm and not the exception.

Many leaders make the mistake of keeping systems the same for many years because they feel like they're working just fine. Why fix something that isn't broken? But when people settle into a routine, autopilot takes over, and this can kill creativity. Autopilot works just fine when you're brushing your teeth, but not so much when you're faced with developing a million dollar project.

ADAPTABILITY DRIVES INVENTION

By using the creative part of your brain, you can make progress, find new solutions, combine different elements, and create new things. This is how people create inventions, by being creative. Many times, inventors develop new ideas by overcoming obstacles or by confronting changing circumstances they weren't prepared for.

This can be seen in the invention of penicillin. Upon returning from holiday in 1928, Alexander Fleming began to inspect petri dishes he had unwittingly left out. The petri dishes contained colonies of *Staphylococcus*, which were growing everywhere except around a small blob of mold, which turned out to be a rare strain of *Penicillium notatum*.

Fleming had not set out to discover penicillin, and if he had refused to adapt to the altered circumstances that the moldy petri dishes presented, he probably never would have. It would have been easy for him to grow frustrated with his mistake and toss all of the moldy dishes into the trash. Instead, he used the opportunity to analyze the effects of his error, which led to the invention of the first antibiotic.

CULTIVATING ADAPTABILITY IN OTHERS

It's good to do things differently each day and to make changes. By being open to changes and challenges, you can find new creative ways to approach your business and life, which will create new neural pathways that prepare you for even greater challenges in the future.

While it's important to improve your own adaptability, as a leader I suggest you also take the time to work on improving it in those around you. By cultivating this skill among your team, you can increase creativity, decrease frustration associated with change, and help everyone get better at finding solutions to problems the business faces.

When you work with a team, occasionally change the environment they work in or the system they're using. You can change how you present materials, how you offer information, or how you communicate. When you present small, unexpected changes, you force your team to be adaptable and to enter a more creative mental space. By offering them the chance to practice adaptability in a controlled way, you prepare them to also be adaptable when faced with larger changes in the company's future.

Communicating Adaptably

Each person will process change at a different speed. This is why it's crucial to adjust how you communicate changes depending on the person you're talking to.

Imagine you have an employee who you will be sending overseas to work at a new office. How can you communicate this change in the best possible way? It's important to first work on connecting with the person. Understanding their current personal circumstances, family situation, and level of motivation at work will help you adapt your approach. For example, if the employee has young children who recently entered school, they will likely struggle with this kind of change, so approaching them in a gentle, understanding way is best. But if they are single and enjoy traveling in their free time, they'll likely see this change as a welcome adventure, and you can approach them more quickly and with enthusiasm.

Creating connections with people is the best way to predict their reactions before a change has been announced. Anticipating a person's reaction and adapting your communication style accordingly will help the individual, as well as the company, when change can't be avoided. Pushing through a change with a communication style that doesn't leave room for discussion or understanding is a sure way to create resistance and resentment, which will decrease both an individual's motivation and sense of belonging in a company.

DIRECT BUT KIND

When communicating a change, do so in a way that leaves room for the other person to make decisions or feel heard. Alan Mulally is one example of a leader who always made sure to speak to his employees with respect and kindness while also being direct. While he admits that it isn't always possible to continue working with someone or to keep an employee on board, he says that it's never necessary to be rude or unkind. For Mulally, even if he were presented with the unpleasant task of firing someone, he would be sure to communicate the fact that he respects the person and everything they brought to the company. In his view, even bad news can come from the heart and be delivered with kindness.

For any leader, it's important to practice kindness when communicating something that someone may not receive in a positive way. It's impossible to hide a decision or change, be it good or bad, so any change should be presented as soon as possible while also keeping each individual's situation and feelings in mind.

LEADING WITH APPRECIATION

The new model of leadership is about appreciating other human beings and their skills. It leaves behind the old idea that leaders are inherently superior and should behave as such. I think we have all seen marriages that have ended amicably, with both sides simply choosing to go in different directions while maintaining mutual respect. The same can happen with employees at any company. It may be time to go separate ways, but when that time comes, it doesn't have to include blame, shame, or a sense of superiority on either side.

In any situation where a change is presented, leading with appreciation is sure to help all team members feel valued and accept changes in a more positive way. For those who are still uncomfortable with a given change, it's important to give them the space to explore that discomfort and overcome it so that they can get fully on board.

For example, imagine if a company that previously worked in multiple languages decides to require that all employees speak and work in English. There will likely be people who feel uncomfortable with the change and find it difficult to adapt. In that case, you as the leader must adapt your approach and engage in discussions. Find out where their discomfort comes from, whether they can imagine getting to a point when they can comply with the change, and what they need to continue to feel valued. This is a moment when you can offer respect through understanding while also communicating what you need in the face of the upcoming change.

By being kind, respectful, and direct, you can ensure that all team members are clear on what is expected from them. At the same time, you're giving them space and time to change because everyone will have different levels of adaptability and will need more or less time to adjust.

For example, being on the film set as a documentary movie producer and director required me to work with different film crews in different countries. Film crews in L.A., San Diego, New York, Switzerland, or Japan operate in different modalities and have a different set of learned work behaviors and expectations. Additionally, each documentary has its own script and set of rules. This means it's very important to be able to communicate with each film crew in a very respectful manner and at the same time be very specific about what I ask for by using simple words understandable to a ten-year-old. In some situations, I needed to be very direct and at the same time careful to not offend people. While filming in Japan during COVID, our gaffer was coughing because he had an allergy. We had eighty people in the room, and I had to respectfully ask him to keep a really low profile and reduce the time he spent with us because people were scared of the coughing.

By connecting with your employees, you can prepare yourself for this and predict how everyone will react and adapt to the new situation you are creating.

Noticing Adaptability in Others

If you are a leader who pays attention, it's possible to notice if and how your team members communicate adaptability.

It's important to recognize that not everyone is adaptable. For example, if you decide to change the location of your meeting from the usual meeting room to a picnic table outside, you may notice that some people shift in discomfort throughout the meeting, aren't paying much attention, or refuse to participate. Others will be enthusiastic, settling in quickly to the new environment, smiling, and participating with renewed energy. The former are likely not very adaptable, while the latter are. The body language and level of engagement are ways people will communicate adaptability.

Beyond body language, you may receive verbal feedback that will help you determine levels of adaptability. Do people voice enthusiasm or ask additional questions to orient themselves? Do they protest or complain?

Once you have done a test with a small, inconsequential change, you will become aware of how they might react to bigger changes. For example, a change in the politics of the company or the discontinuation of a line of products will be a more complex change that will demand more adaptability. Do you think those who were uncomfortable moving the meeting location will take kindly to larger changes like this?

As a leader, I believe putting people on a scale of adaptability can be incredibly helpful when you're seeking to measure the possible response to an upcoming change. Besides changing the location of your next meeting, you can surprise your employees with an unexpected lunch or bring in a consultant to work with your team without offering prior notice. Those who react well to these kinds of changes will be the ones you can count on to adapt quickly when larger changes come along.

Making Your Body Language and Micro Expressions Congruent with Adaptability

At this point, you may think that, as a leader, it can be enough to simply act adaptable in order to get your team on board. But if you don't first get to a point at which you want to accept and welcome change in your life or business, your body language and micro expressions will betray you, letting all of your team members know of your unspoken resistance to the changes you're trying to help them accept.

Congruence—synergy between what you say verbally and your nonverbal communication—is important to convey, and it's also something to keep an eye out for when reading the body language of others. To help with this, we have created the Body Language Congruency Model.

We are looking to see whether the words match the body language. Imagine a timeline of your conversation mapped against the emotional intensity of the verbal language and body

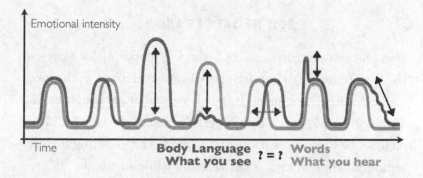

language. If the emotional intensity of the verbal language and the body language always rise at the same time, that's congruent. It's normal for body language to precede words by a second or two, because our reptile brains work faster than our linguistic brains. If someone's body language is much stronger and more intense than what you hear would warrant, this is a sign of incongruence. A classic example of this is someone looking upset and showing micro expressions of sadness or anger but simply saying, "I'm fine."

Imagine you see someone who is very stiff and tense. Their arms are crossed, their lips are pursed, and their eyebrows are knit together. Even if the message they are trying to convey is positive overall, what kind of energy are you receiving from them?

Your having this kind of body language will contradict any positive message you're trying to get across to your team and will contradict your assertion that you're open and willing to tackle the change yourself. That's why it's so important to first work on your own adaptability before expecting others to do so.

HOW WE SAY YES AND NO

I was once working with a CEO who was preparing for a presentation in front of two hundred people about changes in the medical sector in his company. It struck me that even though he had a well-prepared speech that covered many of the benefits of the change, he was subconsciously shaking his head during the presentation. He was saying yes verbally while saying no with his body language.

In general, people are quite good at picking up on body language cues, so of course those in the audience asked him if he really was ready for the change he was presenting about. Realizing that his body language and micro expressions had betrayed him, he confessed his resistance and concerns that the new direction wasn't what was best for the company.

How could he expect everyone else to be enthusiastic about the coming changes if he couldn't yet convince himself of the same?

Before you discuss a change with your team, be honest with yourself about how you feel and, if need be, work through any misgivings you have. Once you have agreed to be part of the change, move forward with it, even if you feel the new direction doesn't align with what you want.

CHANGE WHAT YOU CAN CHANGE

Peter Drucker, an Austrian-American management consultant and educator, and mentor to Goldsmith, once said, "Change what you can change, and accept what you cannot change."

Thinking about changes in a company, you as a leader may have control over some of the changes that come along. But there will be times when you don't have any control over which change is implemented or how. In those cases, it's important to work on accepting the change in order to make sure your body language is congruent with how you're feeling as you present the change to your team.

When you are able to adapt to changes, you'll find that your body language and micro expressions naturally shift. It's important that you also work to create more open body language when possible.

For example, when you speak, work to keep your hands open. When you are showing your wrists, it conveys honesty. Do your best to maintain eye contact. Instead of meeting the eyes of just one or two people, scan the room, briefly catching each person's eyes. When you do this, people will feel more connected to you.

To convey confidence in the face of a change, focus on relaxing your shoulders and offering an occasional smile to convey positivity. When you're relaxed, your gestures will become more fluid and rounded as opposed to being abrupt, which conveys discomfort. Drawing with your hands is a good way to convey comfort in the face of change.

There will likely be a moment when you need to ask your team questions to gauge their level of adaptability regarding a given change. When you do this, ask questions with an open hand instead of pointing. This will subconsciously make them more willing to open up to you. In this way, you can receive valuable feedback about where everyone is and how much work you'll need to do to get everyone on board.

How to Recognize Micro Expressions Using the Wezowski BLINK Technique

As a leader, it can be difficult to get honest or direct answers from your team members. They may not be looking to deceive you, but people are often conditioned to give answers that the questioner wants to hear. This can be detrimental to a company, as problems can be hidden or go unrecognized.

For this reason, it's important to learn how to read micro expressions and body language in order to pick up on cues that can help you see whether your team is genuinely ready to take on a particular change or challenge or whether they are hiding some resistance. The best way to do this is to create a situation where the other person is listening to you, and use that moment to observe them.

When people are listening, they often aren't focused on controlling their own body language or micro expressions. That is where you will be able to observe genuine reactions that aren't being verbalized so as not to upset others.

THE BLINK TECHNIQUE

The BLINK (Body Language Interpretations Nominology Know-How) technique involves presenting a listener with two or more contrasting possibilities or options, recognizing their nonverbal and verbal signs, and reacting to them using carefully chosen statements that clarify for you what they're thinking.

When you do this, you can observe the differing reactions in the person listening to you.

For example, imagine speaking to a team member about a new product line the company wants to implement. You might tell them: "We are planning to implement a new product line. A lot of people at the company are very excited about this. There are going to be complications, but many people are very motivated and excited to solve the problems associated with the new products."

Observe how the person reacts. Do they nod enthusiastically? Do they cross their arms as if protecting themselves? Do they smile or frown? Do their lips curl in contempt? Next, you present them with an opposite option.

You could tell them: "On the other hand, some people at the company are skeptical about the new product line and fear that it won't bring positive results for the company."

Now how do they react? Do they nod as if they understand? Do they crease their brows in frustration? Do they look at the ground?

By watching how they react to each possibility, you can discover which option is more congruent with how they really feel. If they nod enthusiastically when you talk about those who are excited about the new product line, they're likely motivated and ready for the upcoming change. If they cross their arms or frown, they are likely experiencing a sense of resistance to the upcoming change and aren't yet ready to adapt.

THE IMPORTANCE OF FINDING TRUTH SIGNALS

By using the BLINK technique, you can observe truth signals that people will find impossible to hide. By uncovering these truth signals, you can discover who on your team may be resistant to the change you or the company is preparing to implement, and once you do that, you can create a plan that will help get them on board. If those who are resistant are left alone as the change comes about, this could create obstacles during its implementation.

Knowing who is ready for a change and who is not is key in knowing how to best work with your team. Being able to approach those who are not yet ready to adapt and discuss their concerns with them in a direct way can be the difference between your team working together cohesively or falling apart.

BODY LANGUAGE AND MICRO EXPRESSIONS THAT INDICATE OPENNESS	BODY LANGUAGE AND MICRO EXPRESSIONS THAT INDICATE RESISTANCE
• Smiling or nodding	• Crossed arms or legs
• Torso is exposed and turned toward you	• Clenched fists
• Feet pointing toward you	• Feet or torso aimed away from you
• Upper body leans in	• One hand clutching other hand, arm, or elbow

BODY LANGUAGE AND MICRO EXPRESSIONS THAT INDICATE OPENNESS (CONT.)	BODY LANGUAGE AND MICRO EXPRESSIONS THAT INDICATE RESISTANCE (CONT.)
• Happiness micro expression with both lip corners up	• Uneven smile with only one lip corner up (a micro expression of contempt)
• Open arms with palms facing upwards	• Disgust shown with wrinkles around the nose
• Maintaining eye contact around 60 percent of the time	• Anger shown with brows lowered and/or eyelids tightened

Integrating Adaptability Into Who You Are

At the beginning of this chapter, I gave you a few examples of how you can be more adaptable. Here we will dive a bit deeper into how you can integrate adaptability into your essence as a person and receive all of its positive benefits.

THE ROLE OF ADAPTABILITY IN POSITIVE THINKING

Research has found that the majority of people experience many of the same thoughts each day. When we look closely at what people are generally focusing on with their thoughts, we see that many thoughts are related to different negative experiences or emotions in their lives. Fortunately, it's possible to increase the flow of positive thoughts.

People tend to believe that at a certain point our personalities become set in stone, making it impossible to change or grow in any significant way. But Buddhist philosophy teaches that change is possible in every moment of our lives.

MINDFULNESS AND ADAPTABILITY

Matthieu Ricard, author of *Happiness*, puts forward the idea that by becoming aware of our minds and what we are thinking, we can shift our limiting beliefs, which will make us happier. Mindfulness helps to calm our minds and become open to different solutions while minimizing fear and anxiety around change.

Those who lack adaptability tend to experience more fear around the changes they are confronted with. They worry that new things can bring them challenges they are not prepared for, which can cause discomfort and suffering. By discerning these kinds of limiting thoughts around change, you can transform your mind to become more positive and accepting of them.

HOW ADAPTABILITY REDUCES STRESS

Caroline Leaf, author of *Cleaning Up Your Mental Mess: 5 Simple, Scientifically Proven Steps to Reduce Anxiety, Stress, and Toxic Thinking*, dove into clinical research and concluded that only 5–10 percent of diseases come from genetic factors alone, and up to 93 percent of our diseases come from stress. Stress, she found, is often rooted in fear, which can be caused by toxic thought processes, anxiety, and depression. Long-term stress is then allowed to manifest as illnesses, including heart disease, cancer, and more.

That may sound bleak, but it's actually quite a hopeful finding, because if you can learn to manage your stress, you can greatly reduce the possibility of developing common illnesses and ultimately lead a healthier life. To manage your stress, it's important to manage your mind in more productive ways, and much of this comes from being adaptable in the face of challenges.

START WITH SMALL CHANGES

To prepare yourself for challenges and develop more adaptability, it's good to start small. For example, change the kind of toothbrush you use, wear something different to work, take a new route to work, take your partner to a different restaurant, or choose a new dish from the menu.

Once you've practiced implementing small changes, try integrating more complex ones. For example, change your style of communication with your team. Or, instead of having your usual thirty-minute call with your coworker, meet them in a coffee shop. If they live far away, consider calling from the hammock in your backyard instead of from your desk. By creating small challenges for yourself, you can develop more adaptability.

There was a moment when I decided that I needed to develop more adaptability, which required creating a kind of challenge in my life. I was participating in a very intensive course on Thursday mornings and always had to be prepared because we were working through a new project. While the course itself was challenging, I wanted to take it a step further, so one week I decided to do a two-day fast that would start on Wednesday. Normally this would have created stress, as not eating while trying to handle an intensive course was far outside of my comfort zone. But I approached the experience with an open mind and found that I was able to make it through the important one-hour phone call on Thursday, which made me realize my potential to practice adaptability in the face of a less-than-ideal situation. If I could be rational, creative, and focused during a fast, I could certainly do it the following week when I was eating normally. When I realized this, I felt less fearful and more open to changes in my environment, which gave me confidence that I could tap into my best self in the face of change

The point is not to try fasting but simply to challenge yourself to think of how you can create some change in your environment that will push you out of your comfort zone. When you realize that you can still perform well inside of that change, you become more relaxed, open, and confident in your ability to succeed. All of these positive emotions are key in helping you reduce toxic stress and lead a healthier life.

Helping Others Integrate
Adaptability into Their Lives

Let's start with a well-known truth: You can change yourself, but you cannot change others. While many people instinctively know this, they still try to push others into change. This often leads to anger, frustration, or resentment because by pushing them to change, you are suggesting that they are not good enough as they are, and people do not respond well to this.

While you cannot force others to change, as a leader you can lead by example.

I was at lunch with Marshall Goldsmith a couple of years ago. The conversation was flowing from one topic to the next, and at one point, I started talking about healthy eating, which I care deeply about. Marshall paused for a moment and told me that it's good to be an example of healthy eating but not necessarily to preach to others that they should eat healthy because the other person will feel that you are judging them in a negative light. I reflected on this afterward and realized that it often happens that instead of exemplifying the quality we want to change in others through our actions, we find it easier to try to preach to others about why they should change. This is generally ineffective, as it creates resistance to the change you're advocating for.

Therefore, instead of trying to convince others to be adaptable through your words, show them what adaptability looks like through your actions and invite them to be part of your experience. For example, if you want your family to practice adaptability, you can change the kind of music you listen to in the car with them one day. You can find a new local event for all of you to attend. Any kind of surprise will likely be met with enthusiasm and will also create a small change that will invite adaptability.

By sharing in your experiences where adaptability is necessary, others can be transformed and become more adaptable themselves. Actions, not words, will show others what you embody. When you manifest this quality in your life, it has the capability to inspire others to invite it into their own.

CHAPTER TWO

EMPATHY

● ● ● ● ● ● ● ●

Around ten years ago, my friend's mother decided to visit to spend time with her two-year-old granddaughter. My friend went grocery shopping one day, and her mother took her daughter to a local park to play. The little girl soon started crying and was visibly upset. The grandmother, misinterpreting what her granddaughter needed in that moment, tried to play with her and joke with her to no avail.

When my friend got to the park, she watched what was happening and realized that her mother was struggling in a moment that required empathy. The grandmother was unable to connect to her granddaughter's pain, which caused a kind of emotional misalignment. Of course, the grandmother's efforts were doomed to fail.

WHAT PREVENTS EMPATHY

Watching her mother playing with her daughter, my friend realized that not everyone is capable of putting themselves in others' shoes and connecting in emotional situations. She also remembered that her mother had been diagnosed with depression and was likely less able to empathize because the depression was causing an emotional block.

Beyond depression and other mental illnesses, stress and anxiety can cause you to have less capacity for empathy. When your mind is pushing through its own mental limitations, how do you expect to extend empathy and understanding to others?

As a leader, you are likely quite busy. You are working on your own personal goals, which may be causing some level of stress, anxiety, or frustration. Is that getting in the way of your ability to be empathetic? If so, it's important to recognize this and work to shift into a mindset where empathy is possible because it can be a game changer in any company and with any team of employees.

BUILDING CONNECTIONS THROUGH EMPATHY

In the case with my friend's mother, if she had been able to be empathetic, she likely would have been able to help her granddaughter feel better and would have spent the rest of the afternoon playing and enjoying the time with her. There would have been a moment of emotional alignment and connection. The same is true in leadership.

When leaders take the time to practice empathy and get emotionally aligned with their whole team, they gain insights that can be key in leadership. Through empathy, leaders can see moments of upset, stress, and anxiety. They can understand the limitations their team members are facing and work to bring out the full potential of each person without pushing them too far.

THE IMPORTANCE OF COMMUNICATING EMPATHY AS A LEADER

Many leaders have faced multiple challenges during their careers. They've likely overcome these challenges and feel confident in their abilities. This can sometimes make it difficult for them to understand why employees can't simply push forward and overcome a challenge they're facing, but it can also open an opportunity of empathy.

If a leader can tap into their memories and remember what it felt like to confront the first major challenge of their career, they will be more prepared to empathize with the distress of an employee and guide them with effective communication. Without this kind of understanding, the leader may become emotionally incompatible with the team, causing frustration and rifts.

Often, when a leader fails to empathize with team members, the team members will find support in each other. While this can be a good thing for a while as it takes the pressure off the leader, in the end it can lead the team to begin complaining or gossiping behind the leader's back as a way to express their frustration. If this is allowed to go on, it can completely block the progress of a project and undermine the success of a team.

LOOKING AT ORIGINS

Thich Nhat Hanh, a Vietnamese Buddhist monk and philosopher, spoke a great deal about why understanding others is so important. He demonstrated this through a simple example. He would ask his listeners to imagine a plain piece of paper. He would then ask them to consider how the paper had been created and who had been involved. Once upon a time there had been a tree, and then there were people who cut the tree down. Those people then had to transport the tree to a factory, where more workers processed the tree into paper. After that, more people were involved in transporting the paper overseas to its final destination. In the end, there were likely hundreds of people involved in the creation of that single piece of paper.

The point of this example is to demonstrate the importance of origins. Once you remember the tree and the process it goes through to become paper, you look at that piece of paper with a new perspective. The same is true when you look at the origin of any individual.

If you, as a leader, take the time to understand how your team members ended up at your company and what their motivations are in their work, it becomes much easier to lead. When people are treated as having the same origin as everyone else, they feel less motivated to connect with their leader and demonstrate their individual talents. Once you show them that you recognize their uniqueness and empathize with their individual struggles, you create a connection that will manifest as a cohesive team.

BOUNDARIES IN EMPATHY

While it's imperative to offer empathy as a way to connect with your team, it's also important to create boundaries that prevent this empathy from getting in the way of your team's success. If you are empathetic all the time, it can be difficult to manage a team, as individuals learn to take advantage of the constant empathy extended to them. For this reason, it's key to identify situations in which empathy is necessary while also maintaining a sense of authority and determination to carry out your vision.

I have to practice this very thing as a filmmaker. In my work, I make documentaries, which requires filming many interviews that often result in more than a hundred hours of footage. The most difficult task I am faced with is taking the footage and creating a sixty- to ninety-minute documentary. A lot of empathy is involved here, and it could become overwhelming without a sense of perspective.

Each speaker that I interview wants to be visible in the final film. They believe their message to be essential to the success of the documentary and important for those who will watch it. During the interviews, I need to be able to demonstrate empathy in order to understand the speaker and help them share their message in the most authentic way possible. But I must then create some boundaries and take a step back from empathy in order to work on the edits that will become the final film. If I continue to extend empathy to all of the speakers, it would be nearly impossible for me to complete the cuts and edits required to make a comprehensive yet concise documentary. Each speaker may only be featured for a few minutes, and I need to be able to distance myself from any disappointment they feel if I am to complete my work. There are moments when I need to consider an individual's feelings and others when I need to focus on the success of the project as a whole. Boundaries are what allow me to do that.

Creating boundaries as a leader allows you to connect with team members by extending understanding while also taking a step back when it's required in order to think of the team as a whole and the decisions that need to be made. For a leader, decision-making is part of your responsibilities, and while empathy should play a role, you cannot allow it to prevent you and your team from moving forward.

How to Recognize Empathy in Yourself and Others

When you meet someone new, what do you talk to them about? Do you find yourself sharing details of your family and work? Do you discuss your opinions on recent world or local events? Or do you take the time to ask them what they do for work, if they have children, or what they thought of that recent newsworthy moment?

If you tend to dominate a conversation with details of yourself and your life, this may be a sign that you lack empathy. Forgetting to ask others about themselves is a sure sign that you have room to grow when it comes to this particular trait. If you have heard people describe you as stubborn, arrogant, or overbearing, this can also be another signal that you lack empathy, as these words generally point to a lack of consideration for others.

The idea here is to cultivate the opposite.

HOW TO PRACTICE EMPATHY

Being empathetic, as we mentioned before, involves being able to put yourself in someone else's shoes in order to consider what they may be feeling or experiencing. To practice this, I want to suggest a simple role play.

Imagine a moment when you need to make a decision affecting an employee or team member at your company. Place one chair on the floor to represent you, positioning it across from a second chair that represents your employee. Also place a third chair off to the side to represent a "third party."

First, sit in your own chair and think about how you see the situation from your own perspective. How does the upcoming decision make you feel? Will it change anything about your job or your relationship to your coworkers and team members?

Next, sit in the chair that represents your employee. Try to put yourself in their position, receiving news of the decision that is to be made. How are they likely to feel about it? What will the experience change in their work? Will it be positive or negative for them? If this person has skills or a background that is very different from yours, this exercise could be difficult at first, but even taking the time to consider what they *might* think or feel is a great way to begin practicing empathy.

For the final part of the exercise, sit in the third chair. We spoke before about the importance of being able to see a situation as a whole without feeling too personally connected to the outcome, as this allows you to make decisions that are best for both the company and your team members. While sitting in the third chair, this is an opportunity to practice just that. Here, you are taking in the perspectives of both yourself and your employee without feeling too deeply invested in either. Consider the overall situation and how it will affect everyone involved.

HOW TO RECOGNIZE A GROWING SENSE OF EMPATHY

Once you start to practice empathy with the kind of exercise described, you should notice that your capacity for empathy begins to grow. What exactly will that look like?

You may notice that you ask people how they are, what's going on in their life, what projects they are dealing with at work, or even, simply, how their day is going. These kinds of questions indicate empathy, as it shows you are making space for their feelings and thoughts. The more you do this, the more skillful you will become with empathy.

I was once invited to lunch with Alan Mulally. I was one of eight other people sitting at the table, and what amazed me about Alan was his sense of empathy. Even with so many people, he made sure everyone was given space to speak and share their thoughts. There was a moment where two of the guests were sharing a great deal and taking up more of the talking space. During a break in the conversation, Alan took a moment to ask me about my opinion on what was being discussed. Many people wouldn't have taken the time to notice that I hadn't shared much and may have appreciated the chance to do so.

Taking the time to offer someone a glass of water when they enter your office or asking how they are before discussing the topic of the meeting can go a long way in putting your employees at ease so that they feel heard and respected.

Simple displays of empathy such as this can make a big difference in how your team members relate to you.

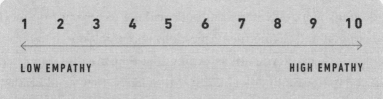

1   2   3   4   5   6   7   8   9   10

← ——————————————————————————— →

LOW EMPATHY   HIGH EMPATHY

This is a scale you can use to measure the empathy of each member of your team and then discuss what may need to be improved. For example, if Norma was the least empathetic according to group results, what tips can all of you give her to be more empathetic? You can also use this to measure a leader's empathy and give them feedback.

How to Verbally Communicate
Empathy to Others

I gave some examples in the previous section regarding why it's important to show interest in others. Now, how can you show that interest verbally? The key lies in asking questions.

When you speak to someone, take the time to ask them questions related to what they enjoy or are interested in. For example, you may be a golf enthusiast, but speaking to anyone you meet about golf and asking them questions about golf doesn't convey empathy because you are assuming that they are also interested in golf and want to talk about it. More likely, they would rather talk about something else, but how will you know if you don't ask? Empathy is about being interested in what the other person is interested in, if only for a moment.

I remember once spending an hour with someone who was talking about dogs. He had a bull terrier that he was very enthusiastic about, to say the least. He went on and on about his bull terrier and about training and keeping dogs. Not once did he ask me if I was interested in dogs, if I had a dog, or even whether I liked animals. He did not take the time to understand how much his topic of interest would resonate with me, displaying a deep lack of empathy.

The point is to make sure that when you begin a conversation, try to discuss something that is interesting or relevant to both you and the person you're speaking to. Ask pertinent questions to discover possible topics or directions to take the conversation. This will help you practice empathy while also ensuring that both parties enjoy the other's company.

HOW TO DISCOVER TOPICS OF CONVERSATION THAT ARE RELEVANT TO OTHER PEOPLE

No one is a mind reader, of course, and simply guessing at topics of conversation that you think others will find interesting often isn't effective. A better way to go about it would be to start asking open-ended questions that will help you discover what they like or need.

For example, you can ask them what they enjoy talking about; what their current interests are; whether they like music or sports; what kinds of books and movies they enjoy; or what projects they are currently working on. Questions starting with "what" are generally safe, open questions that will help you uncover good places to begin a fulfilling conversation with someone.

What if you want to understand another person emotionally? There are also relevant questions you can ask here to get the lay of the land. Here, try using "how" questions. For example, you can ask how they are feeling today; how interested they are in their current hobbies; how they feel about the projects they're participating in at work; or how they're liking working with their current team members. If the other person seems reluctant to dive too deep into their feelings, you can gently prompt them with phrases that start with "Tell me more." This demonstrates your interest in and openness to what they want to share.

THE IMPORTANCE OF CREATING SPACE

Leaders are busy people, and they often become accustomed to rushing through conversations. This doesn't necessarily mean that they lack empathy, but it may mean that they unintentionally close spaces where empathy could thrive.

As a leader, if you need something done, you likely convey the message and move on to the next thing to avoid wasting time. Even if you do take the time to ask questions, are you offering enough space for the person to respond in a meaningful way, or are you leading the conversation to be quick or abrupt with your body language or facial expressions? Leaders tend to be action takers, which can leave little room to also be listeners. This can create the impression that you don't care about the people you are speaking with, as it doesn't convey empathy.

If you want to cultivate empathy, you must create space. When you ask someone an open question, take a deep breath, and give them space to speak and share their feelings and ideas. Even if you feel that they have finished speaking, offer an extra pause, as this can sometimes prompt them to share more. When you pace yourself in this way, you are creating the space that is needed for the other person to communicate what they think or feel. In those spaces, you can create genuine connections and receive information that can help you better relate to and manage your team.

How to Notice if Others Are Communicating Empathy

How do you know if others are offering you empathy? It is very important to recognize when this is happening, as you will then be able to reciprocate or thank them for taking the time to care about what you are thinking or how you are feeling. It takes time and effort to be empathetic, so recognizing when someone is doing this for you is key, as you will then feel more connected and appreciative.

If one of your team members were to come up to you after a business trip and ask you how your trip was, this would demonstrate empathy on their part. In that case, it would be a perfect moment to thank them for asking, as they will then also feel appreciated. The mutual positive feelings created in this interaction can strengthen a sense of connection and loyalty.

A friend once came to stay at my house for a few days, and we decided to go to the beach one day. When we returned, my friend hung her beach towel on the terrace. That evening, I adjusted the towel and added some pegs to keep it from blowing away during the night. The next evening, I noticed that my friend hung her towel in the way I had the day before. This may not seem like a big gesture, but it indicates a deep sense of empathy. My friend had taken the time to notice that I had changed how the towels were hung and then made sure to copy this the next evening to make things easier and more convenient for me. I had invited her into my home, and she returned that kindness by demonstrating empathy in how she interacted with my space.

You may see this happen with a coworker, as well. For example, if a coworker asks for your help with a project, empathy would suggest that you take the time to notice how they are tackling pieces of the project and try to do it in a similar way in order to keep things organized and consistent for them. It's a subtle gesture but one that they are sure to be grateful for.

BODY LANGUAGE AND MICRO EXPRESSIONS THAT INDICATE EMPATHY	BODY LANGUAGE AND MICRO EXPRESSIONS THAT SUGGEST A LACK OF EMPATHY
• Stable eye contact	• Looking away
• Open palms	• Closed or rapid gestures
• Relaxed posture	• Covering face by scratching or touching
• Chest forward	• Body turned away, distracted posture
• Sitting comfortably in chair	• Nose wrinkled in disgust
• Happiness micro expression with both lip corners up	• Smiling in contempt with only one lip corner up

OMOTENASHI

Kindness is very closely related to empathy, and people who cultivate empathy tend to have more capacity for kindness, as well. This can be seen in the Japanese concept of *omotenashi*, which means to wholeheartedly look after guests. It's a kind of genuine and selfless hospitality that permeates into almost every aspect of Japanese culture. In *omotenashi*, there is a deep-rooted desire to make others comfortable, whether they are customers, guests, clients, or friends. Those who offer *omotenashi* give without expecting anything in return, and this hospitality is present in all moments of everyday life, from high-stakes business interactions to informal get-togethers with friends.

There's a Japanese proverb that says, "One kind word can warm three winter months." The concept of *omotenashi* revolves around genuine, selfless kindness. In these moments of kindness, you are pausing to forget about yourself and consider the needs and wants of others, which evolves into empathy.

Omotenashi is firmly rooted in the cultural history of the tea ceremony. This ceremony is an elaborate offering of hospitality that aims to create a harmonious atmosphere between those who have gathered. Each act of service, however small, sparks a moment of happiness and connection in an otherwise busy life and goes a long way in creating a sense of harmony between yourself and others. This begins to get to the root of why empathy is so vital for any leader.

The moments when someone holds a door open for you or makes your coffee just the way you like it are about both empathy and kindness. Both of these concepts stem from a sense of momentary selflessness. Small kindnesses will be remembered, and the empathy that occurs from there can help to build a bridge and create powerful relationships with others.

GIVING YOUR FULL ATTENTION

You likely find it easy to notice when someone is giving you their full attention, and when they aren't. Empathy demands full attention in order for it to blossom. The simple act of listening can indicate that you care about what the other person is saying and vice versa. If someone takes the time to listen to you, you feel that they empathize with you.

I experience this constantly with my children. I have two children, ages five and seven, and when I take the time to give them my full attention, even if only for one minute, I find that they are able to relax and be more independent in the moments that follow. If I fully give them that one minute, they feel heard and fulfilled, which can carry throughout the whole day. This is the power of attention and can work with anyone, from your partner to your team members to your boss.

When you offer your full attention to someone, you can quickly learn what they need or want and can empathize with that. Listening is a simple act that is both healing and transforming. When you ask someone how they feel, how they're doing at work, or how their family is, keep an open mind when listening to their answers. In this way, a moment of listening transforms into a moment of empathy.

How to Use Your Body Language and Micro Expressions to Be Congruent with Empathy

MIRRORING

Mirroring is one of the most important skills you can develop as you're working toward a greater sense of empathy. Mirroring is essentially copying the body language of the person you are interacting with. For example, if you observe two people, you may notice that if one has their arms crossed, the other person may cross their arms a few moments later. They may even do this subconsciously.

Mirroring is so key in empathy because if your body language does not align with the person you are interacting with, they may feel isolated or misunderstood, and disagreements may ensue more easily. To cultivate understanding, observe the body language of the other person, and do your best to copy it. If they put their hands in their pockets, do the same. If they have their legs crossed, do the same.

Now, if the body language of the other person is negative, for example, if they are crossing their arms or turning their body away from you, try to mirror them slightly less. You could cross your arms, but try not to turn your body away. After a few minutes, you can begin to insert more positive, open body language, such as opening your palms, relaxing your shoulders, or making eye contact. Move between mirroring and inserting more open body language. Eventually, they will probably begin to mirror you and the open body language you have presented. If you can achieve this, you can help guide the conversation in a more productive direction by getting everyone onto the same page.

MATCHING ENERGY

With body language, it's also important to match the other person's energy. I travel often, and in Italy, I encounter many people who are very expressive and energetic. They use their hands, move their bodies, and use a greater vocal range when speaking. In that environment, I try to increase my energy to get as close as possible to theirs so that they feel comfortable with me and the conversation.

On the other hand, when I go to Norway or Denmark, I often find myself conversing with people who are more reserved and more deliberate with what they say. Here, I have to work to slow down my speech in order to match their pace and the rhythm of their body language. It's like a dance. If you have any experience dancing with multiple partners, you know that you must adjust the way you dance depending on your partner. If you engage in the dance of mirroring correctly, you can create empathy that flows from both sides.

The most important element here is developing the ability to remain engaged in a conversation while also noticing what the other person is doing with regards to their body language and micro expressions. If you notice a shift in their body language, shift with them. For example, if they suddenly begin to indicate sadness through micro expressions, settle into your own micro expressions of sadness as a way of subconsciously indicating that you understand what they are feeling. This will help you as a leader create space for discussions where your team members feel safe and heard.

How to Recognize Empathy in Body Language and Micro Expressions Using the BLINK Technique

The BLINK conversation technique is also very important when speaking about empathy because this is how you can discover more about others' preferences. Imagine, for example, that you want to take your partner out to dinner. Instead of taking them to the usual place that you always go, you want to surprise them. But instead of surprising them with something they may not like, you can present various options and use the BLINK technique to discern which they prefer.

You may say: "Honey, tonight how about we try something new? I heard about this new restaurant with live music, great cocktails, and a dance floor. Also some friends of ours went out to a French place where the food comes out in a number of small courses, and they have a huge wine list. There's also that cozy sushi place we've been meaning to try. . . ."

As you present the three options to your partner, you would use the BLINK technique to observe their body language and micro expressions. When do they express enthusiasm or happiness? Do they make more eye contact when you're presenting the first option? Do they smile slightly when you mention sushi? Do they crease their eyebrows in uncertainty when you talk about French food? By noticing when they begin to lean forward, pay more attention, or suggest excitement with their micro expressions, you can deduce where they would like to go for dinner.

The option for empathy then naturally follows. Perhaps you were more excited about going to a place where dancing was an option, but your partner has suggested to you that they prefer sushi. Here, you can use empathy to follow their preference. If you have offered them options, respect the choice they have chosen through the BLINK technique.

THE BLINK TECHNIQUE AND KINDNESS

By using the BLINK technique for these kinds of situations, you create space for kindness. When you deduce what restaurant your partner wants to go to, an act of kindness follows when you take them to that restaurant.

As a leader, you can use this with your coworkers, employees, or team members, as well. For example, you can use the BLINK technique in a similar way to discover how your coworker takes their coffee. It will be a nice surprise for them, then, when you bring them exactly what they wanted the next day. If you're working on writing a report with your team members, offer options about what could be included in the report. For example, you could say: "Would you rather have a descriptive report with a lot of details included, would you go more for a lot of statistics and graphs, or would you rather focus on experience with the customers and what you learned from conversations with them?"

Then use the BLINK technique to discern what they feel is important and should be included. This can lead to satisfactory work for all parties involved.

Kindness comes from creating space for more than one option instead of pressuring others into your preferred choice. By observing others' reactions and fulfilling what is important for them, you can use the BLINK technique to create more empathy.

●

How to Integrate Empathy
into Who You Are

When I was twenty, I got a job in a coffee shop in Cardiff, Wales. After some time working there, I became a manager overseeing several employees. One day, one of my employees made several mistakes while delivering food to customers, and the final straw was when she tried to give dumplings to a customer who had requested lasagna. I became very upset with the employee and told her that she needed to eat the dumplings for lunch since she made the mistake. Overwhelmed by the bustle and stress of the position I was in as a manager, I was unable to practice empathy in this situation.

Being harsh and rude to this particular employee didn't bring any kind of positive outcome. The employee felt worse about her mistake, and my actions harmed the relationship we had as manager and employee. I see now that what I could have done instead was to create space for empathy. In that situation, empathy may have included taking her aside and asking her what I could do to help her or what she needed in that moment in order to focus more on what the customers were telling her. It could have been as simple as offering her a five-minute break from her duties or simply listening to her talk about the struggles she was facing that day.

THE LONG-TERM BENEFITS OF CREATING
SPACE FOR EMPATHY

It often feels like extra work for leaders when you have to run a company or a team and are then trying to create space for people to have conversations with you and to listen to their experiences. This extra time and effort, however, can be beneficial in the long run. Not only will it make you a more empathetic person in general, but you can build deeper relationships with others when you make space for empathy.

As a leader, you've likely created certain systems within your team, and empathetic actions may force you outside the comfort zone that those systems have created. Perhaps you see that one team member is overwhelmed in their role and needs less responsibility for the next few weeks. This, however, may mess up the system you've created and force you to take the time to reorganize things. This will feel like an inconvenience, but by allowing the overwhelmed team member a bit of respite, you can help them increase their overall productivity while also feeling like a valued member of the team in the long run.

When you learn to pay attention to the needs of your employees and team members, you'll find that they extend the same kindness to you. The new dynamic that is created from this will develop into a more productive way of working together. As I mentioned in chapter 1, the model is no longer a boss dictating orders to their employees. It's about coworking and creating a team that works well together.

I see this dynamic often with my children. I will sometimes go into the kitchen to find flour spattered over the floor, dough sticking to the countertops, and water dripping from the edge of the sink as they attempt to make a cake. If I were to walk in and start barking orders, telling them to clean up their mess, they would likely resist and become resentful. They were just trying to have a little fun, after all. If, instead, I go into the kitchen and offer them the option of working as a team to clean up, they are likely to see it as an opportunity to connect with each other and with me. They feel valued in that moment and are more likely to help in similar situations in the future. The latter requires more effort on my end, as I have to participate in the cleaning, but the work goes quicker and smoother overall, and I have then prepared my children to be more helpful in the future.

This is a simple example that also works in companies. The idea is that helping everyone to feel like they are equally important in a team and taking the time to understand their needs and struggles creates a meaningful bond. This bond will become more and more beneficial in the long term, as it will increase team members' motivations and push them to make more progress together. In the end, they will feel like your success is their success.

How to Help Others Integrate Empathy into Their Lives

Many people tend to wait for someone else to make the first move when it comes to empathy. They think that if someone isn't showing them respect or kindness, then they shouldn't have to do the same. As a leader, it's important not to think this way and to be the one to take the first step in order to create a positive example for those around you.

When you take the time to ask your team members how they are and really listen to their response, it may push them, consciously or unconsciously, to do the same with you or with other team members. Here, mirroring comes back into play. Imagine you're meeting with a client who is resisting your attempts to move forward with a deal. You start mirroring their body language and wording patterns and then start acting a little more positive than they are, asking questions and making summaries that show that you empathize with them. If they say, "This costs more than my company can afford," you could say, "It looks like the fee is expensive. At the same time, do you think that there could be added value to paying our higher fee?" All the while, keep mirroring the body language of the other person.

When you speak with your team members, keeping your body language slightly more open than theirs will help them start to open up more, as well. The next day, instead of simply responding "Fine" when you ask them how they are, they may open up about a tough situation they've been going through recently.

THE ROLE OF CURIOSITY IN EMPATHY

It may not always be the case that empathy results in changing the behaviors of others. Some people may take much longer to open up and feel connected to those around them, but that should not deter you from your practice of empathy. When I spoke about the Japanese concept of *omotenashi*, I mentioned that this comes from a sense of selflessness. The Japanese do not offer kindness because they expect something in return. They offer it because they wish to connect with others. There is a sense of curiosity that is involved in empathy. It involves setting aside your ego and your end goal in order to focus for a moment on the feelings of another human being. This may not always result in reciprocal empathy, but it will not go unnoticed, and more often than not, you will find that offering empathy leads to more empathy being shown toward you.

In your practice of empathy, it can often help to tap into the kind of curiosity that children experience. As adults, we have our own agenda, goals, and worries, which can distract us from those around us and lead us to simply not care about creating connections with others. We become so busy and preoccupied that we simply don't have time to care. Here is where curiosity comes into play, as it can help you shift your mindset. You can't care about everything or everyone, but you can use curiosity to create short moments where you pay attention to others because you are genuinely interested in them.

This is similar to the tea ceremonies in Japan. These are short moments that the Japanese use to put aside their worries and their ego in order to bring other people into their circle and offer them their full attention. Being in the present moment and engaging with those participating in the ceremony creates a moment of connection that extends far beyond those few minutes. The same can happen with your team members. Taking even five or ten minutes to become curious about an individual employee and fully engage in a conversation with them can help them stay motivated and more willing to go the extra mile for their team and the company.

CHAPTER THREE

ENGAGEMENT

● ● ● ● ● ● ● ●

As a leader, you have the power to define the kind of energy that exists at your organization and within your team. Engagement is what helps you do this.

Imagine working on a specific project. Often, the project first requests your attention. You must think about it and make plans to carry it out. Next, you will need to give energy to the project to get the various parts moving. Once you have attention and energy, you can develop engagement. This may include bringing your team together to brainstorm or decide on each person's role. When you become engaged, you can breathe life into an activity. This is what leads to progress.

Engagement cannot exist without attention and focus. If you've ever had a garden, you know that if you engage with it—water the plants, pull the weeds, and so on—your plants will grow. But if you simply pay attention to it by observing it, or offer limited energy by watering the plants sporadically, wild species will take over, killing your beloved plants.

When you pay attention, you create awareness, which opens you to changes in behavior as well as creative input from others. From attention and awareness, focus can develop. It's the sense of focus and interest in an activity that can lead to engagement.

Engagement is what creates cooperation in a company. By being engaged as a leader, you can show your team members and employees that you care about them and what they do at the company. When your team members feel that you have their back, they will develop greater motivation.

THE LIMITS OF ENGAGEMENT

Leaders tend to think that if they practice engagement, they need to do the same amount of work on each particular project as their employees. This, of course, doesn't work for many leaders. Leaders have their own responsibilities and need the space to delegate work in order to open time for the decision-making and planning that they must do. Engagement does not demand that leaders put all of their responsibilities to the side in order to be constantly involved with your team members' work. It means that you remain open to questions and requests while maintaining a positive energy that will serve as an example for your team.

As a leader, you can be engaged without depleting your resources. When you practice being open and interested in your team members' work, you become engaged, and this energy is what will motivate others. Even engaging with your employees for ten minutes each day may be enough to demonstrate your interest. As long as you remain open to stepping in when your input and energy are needed, you are practicing engagement.

●

What Causes Leaders to Limit Engagement

Engagement depends on your attitude and your energy. You can check in with your sense of engagement by doing a simple thought analysis. When you wake up in the morning, what do you feel as you begin to think about your work and the day ahead of you? Do you experience resistance, fear, or anxiety? Do you experience joy, enthusiasm, or interest? If you find that the former comes to mind first, you may have some work to do in the area of engagement.

There are a few things that may be limiting your ability to engage with your work and your team members. I've listed a few that follow. If any of these resonate with you, there's room for improvement.

DEPRESSION

Depression often causes your thoughts to flow inward, while engagement demands that they flow outward. In this way, depression often creates resistance to engagement, as those struggling with these kinds of negative emotions and thought patterns struggle to create the kind of positive energy that is required in engagement.

STRESS

When you are overwhelmed by your workload, family obligations, or person struggles, your brain will enter a high beta state. As I mentioned in chapter 1, this can block creative thinking and focus, which will limit your ability to engage.

FEAR OF VULNERABILITY

As a leader, if you engage with others and get close to them on a more personal level, you will likely have to experience vulnerability. You will share your strengths and likely reveal your weaknesses as you work alongside those who are specially trained in certain areas. If you have been at a company for twenty years, you will likely have to defer to the knowledge of those who are much younger in some technical matters. That can be difficult for some leaders, as it requires that you be vulnerable and open to learning.

SENSE OF SUPERIORITY

Another factor that can block engagement is a sense of superiority. If you believe yourself to be better than your employees, that can get in the way of your openness to engaging with them. If you talk to them from a place of superiority, you can unconsciously limit cooperation and decrease the motivation your team members feel. In the end, when employees don't feel respected or appreciated, they will begin to come to work only for a paycheck, as they will stop caring about the company and their team's success.

VULNERABILITY AND ENGAGEMENT

In *The Earned Life*, Hubert Joly, a former CEO of Best Buy, discusses the importance of vulnerability in leadership. He says that one of the most important things he learned in working with Marshall Goldsmith was the importance of not only getting to know his employees but letting his employees get to know him on a personal level. It's important, he says, to admit when you're struggling with a problem and ask for input from the team members around you. "It's one of the strengths of leadership," he says.

Vulnerability flows from the way you communicate with those around you. Being open to sharing your strengths and weaknesses, as well as inviting others to communicate the same to you, is what helps create a sense of kinship within a team. By being open in the way you communicate, you can invite team members who are skilled in an area to step in where others may be weaker. That, in fact, is the main function of a team—to bring various skill sets together to create a cohesive whole. By sitting down with your employees to brainstorm, share problems, explore solutions, and make decisions, you can practice engagement and get the most out of each person.

How to Recognize Engagement in Yourself and Others

As I mentioned before, a perfect time to check in on your level of engagement is when you wake up in the morning. When you think about work, consider the feelings and thoughts that come to mind. You can even consider your engagement on a scale of 1–10, where 1 would represent a very weak sense of engagement. You would feel reluctant to go to work, and the thoughts around the projects you will need to face during the day would be largely negative. Ten would represent a very strong sense of engagement. You would feel enthusiastic about the day ahead and excited to work with your team members on the projects you're currently involved in.

You can also use this kind of scale to check in with your employees. But how do you gauge their level of engagement? Here, communication comes into play. Ask them about the tasks they are working on. How do they feel about them? Are they exploring solutions to certain problems? Are their thoughts elsewhere?

If you find that you or your employees are experiencing low engagement, it's important to uncover the reasons for this.

There are many things that can cause individuals or teams to disengage with the work in front of them. Some of these are outside or environmental factors, while others may have to do more with their state of mind. Here are some factors that can cause low engagement.

LACK OF INFORMATION

One thing that can cause someone to not be fully engaged is a simple lack of information. If you are facing a task but haven't been given enough instructions or direction about what's expected of you, you're likely to feel overwhelmed and unsure, which can quickly lead to disengagement.

LACK OF SKILLS

If you give a team member a task that doesn't match their skill set, they may be unable to fully engage with it. If they lack the skills to complete the task or project in the correct way, they won't feel confident in their abilities. This can extend beyond the task itself and seep into other areas of their work.

FEAR OF NOT BEING GOOD ENOUGH

Many people need to receive at least occasional confirmation that they are doing a good job. If the leader is not providing that, individual employees may begin to lack confidence and disengage from their work. Even if they have the skills and information needed to complete what is in front of them, if they feel that their leader doesn't believe in them or the work they're doing, their motivation and confidence can lower.

PERSONAL DIFFICULTIES

Every leader and employee is living a unique life with its own related struggles. A team member may be experiencing something difficult in their personal life that is causing them to become distracted or disengaged at work. While they may try to compartmentalize in order to do their work well, it isn't always possible. In these cases, it is important to check in with the individual to see what kind of support they need. If they do not feel supported, their lack of engagement can become a long-term problem.

Several years ago, I was working with a high-level engineer at a company producing cars. During that time, he sadly lost his son to leukemia. He was understandably out of sorts and was unable to work for several months. At that moment, it was important to find a solution that worked for him as an individual and for the company as a whole. He was integral to the work being done, so the leaders around him did what they could to offer him temporary leave while preserving his position at the company for the time when he was ready to return.

In this case, if the company had simply turned a blind eye to his personal struggles, he would likely have become very unhappy with his position and the company he was working for. Engagement would have become increasingly difficult for him. Fortunately, the leaders at the company took his situation into consideration and found a solution that worked for everyone.

ATTITUDE OF THE LEADER

As I mentioned before, employees feed off the energy of their leader. Therefore, if a leader is disengaged and doesn't seem to care what their team members are doing, this can inhibit the engagement of everyone around them.

Twelve years ago, I was working as a coach with nineteen departments of a bank. Each department had its own manager, and during my time working with them, it quickly became obvious which managers were more present and engaged. Those departments had teams that were more engaged overall and were experiencing better results in sales and performance. I noticed that even when a manager was absent for just a week or two due to illness, that short absence caused team engagement to reduce. There was no contingency plan in place to ensure that someone was able to step in for an absent leader.

At any company, it's important to ensure that there is always a leader present and that the leader is prepared to take on their work with a positive attitude and a strong sense of engagement.

LACK OF BELIEF IN A PROJECT

Individuals want to feel fulfilled in the work that they do. If they are working at a company or on a project that they don't believe in or that doesn't feel important, they may become resistant to the work. This often happens with those in customer service who are faced with inconsiderate customers on a daily basis. If the employee is feeling constantly attacked and unsupported, they become disengaged and resentful.

With any new project that you give to your team members, it's important to receive verbal confirmation from them regarding their commitment to the work. You can ask them directly if they are ready to take on the project. Listen to any concerns they have and take them seriously. If you cannot get to a place where the team member says, "Yes, I'm ready," then it may be time to step back to take a look at any other issues that may be behind their resistance.

LEARNED HELPLESSNESS

In the 1960s, Martin E. P. Seligman and Steven F. Maier conducted an experiment using two groups of dogs. In one group, the dogs received electrical shocks that they could not control. In the other group, the dogs could end the shocks by pressing a lever. It shouldn't be hard to guess which group of dogs showed signs of anxiety and depression. Interestingly, even when the first group was given the opportunity to escape the shocks later in the experiment, they didn't. The researchers called this phenomenon "learned helplessness."

What do dogs have to do with your team members? Well, a great deal. Imagine giving an employee an extensive project and telling them they have twenty-four hours to complete it. The first time, they will likely feel stressed but will attempt to do it, even though they know it will be impossible. If this happens over and over, they will become disengaged, experience a lack of motivation, and decide that it isn't worth it to try to finish the project in the allotted time because the leader will be unhappy with whatever they do; that is, they will develop learned helplessness.

The idea is to give your individual team members responsibility and control over some aspects of what they are doing. When they feel they have some control over the process and outcome, they will feel more engaged and motivated to present a good final product.

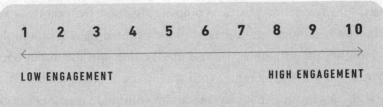

| 1 | 2 | 3 | 4 | 5 | 6 | 7 | 8 | 9 | 10 |

LOW ENGAGEMENT   HIGH ENGAGEMENT

This is a scale you can use to measure the engagement of each member of your team and then discuss what may need to be improved. For example, if Bill was the least engaged according to group results, what tips can all of you give him to be more engaged? You can also use this to measure a leader's engagement and give them feedback.

How to Verbally Communicate Engagement to Others

Conveying a sense of engagement is rooted in caring. If you want to show those around you that you are engaged, it's important to show them that you care about who they are, what they are doing, and what they need moving forward.

USING "WE"

When communicating a sense of engagement, it's important to stress collaboration. You can do this by using "we" and "us" instead of "I" or "you." For example, leaders will often say, "I want you to complete this task by tomorrow." Instead, you could say, "It's important that we complete this task by tomorrow so that we can move onto the next phase of the project." By simply changing the pronouns you use and getting specific about why you need something done, you convey more engagement. You are demonstrating that you care about your team member's time and energy while also acknowledging the importance of the work at hand, as well as their role in the team.

While it's not always possible to use "we" when speaking, it's important to help your team feel that they are working together. When you show them results, present progress, and use language that reminds them that others are depending on them, it can create more engagement and motivation.

MOTIVATIONAL LANGUAGE

When it comes to engagement, it's also important to employ motivational or inspirational language. This often takes the form of compliments or acknowledging the work that someone has done. For example, you can say, "I have confidence that you are capable of completing this task" or "I really like the way you put this plan together." These are simple phrases that can do a great deal to bolster your employees' motivation and self-esteem. When your team feels that you believe in, trust, and appreciate them, they will have more confidence, which can develop into greater engagement.

CONVEYING CONFIDENCE

The energy you give to your speech when speaking to your team is another thing that will convey your engagement (or lack of). Take the time to notice how you formulate sentences about the project or task at hand. If your energy is sluggish or disinterested, your team members may feel that you are not committed to the goal you hope to fulfill. Your tone of voice, vocabulary, and facial expressions can all add to the positive or negative energy you offer.

It's important to use your energy to convey confidence in what you are asking your employees to do. If you do not believe in your team or in the project you've given them, they will begin to waver. People need to hear decisive, clear language in order to feel confident going forward.

Consider the following directions from a leader: "We need to finish the editing stage of the movie within the next three months. Let's start with going through the editing of the short scenes and making sure all of the words are important. Then, we will focus on the images and cutting out the unnecessary elements. Finally, we will work on the sounds and music."

If you received these directions from a leader, you would likely feel confident in the direction you should go from there. You know the goal and the steps you must take to get there.

Now, consider these directions: "I think we should complete the editing of the movie within the next three months. If we don't, I'm afraid we won't have enough time to complete additional edits before the date of the film festival. If we're too close to the deadline, I worry that there will be lots of editing mistakes, and that could make our investors angry. I'm not sure if three months is realistic, but let's get started and see how it goes."

How would you feel after receiving these instructions? Probably not very positive. Not only does the leader seem unsure of the goal and the plan, but they are using phrases like "I'm afraid" and "I worry." Fear, uncertainty, hesitancy, and anger are all present, which combine to create a very negative energy that will leave the team member feeling a lack of confidence in what they should be doing and when.

As a leader, it's imperative to demonstrate certainty, clarity, and confidence. If you aren't feeling sure about a plan or a project, hold off on passing on instructions to your team. Take the time to work through any obvious problems that you see, and when you have a clear plan in front of you, take it to your team so that they can begin working with confidence and dedication.

If you find later that your original plan isn't panning out, lay out how your team can move forward from that point while clarifying the new goal. Changes are fine as long as you, as the leader, are open and feel confident about the team's short- and long-term goals.

How to Notice if Others Are Verbally Communicating Engagement

As we discussed in the previous section, enthusiasm is conveyed through both your words and energy. When you want to figure out if someone is engaged, listen for positive or negative feelings conveyed through the vocabulary they choose. If someone is engaged, you will often hear phrases like:

- I'm happy with . . .
- I'm enjoying . . .
- I'm convinced that . . .
- I'm sure . . .
- I can confirm . . .

All of these phrases demonstrate positive feelings, commitment, and motivation. Of course, it also depends on the energy they give to their speech. Pay attention to whether they are using positive, active, vibrant energy, as this demonstrates engagement and is something that is easily recognized and felt.

On the contrary, if someone isn't engaged, you may hear them start sentences with phrases like:

- I'm afraid . . .
- I'm anxious about . . .
- I'm stressed about . . .

- I'm not sure . . .
- I doubt . . .
- I don't know . . .

If you notice that someone is expressing doubt or uncertainty, quick intervention is necessary. This may indicate a sense of helplessness, which could be connected to learned helplessness, as we discussed earlier. If there is a sense of helplessness, it may mean that the team member is feeling unsupported, unsure, or unconfident. They are likely trying to do their work but may not be getting great results. For that reason, it's important to listen for signs of negative feelings or energy.

CLEARING BLOCKAGES

While it's important to check in with what people are saying directly to you, it's also important to tap into what your employees or team members may be saying behind your back. Many times, employees will not go directly to their leader with doubts or frustrations as they fear backlash. This can lead them to share their frustrations with their coworkers and become passive-aggressive in their job. Of course, this will create negative energy and lower engagement and motivation. Gossip can create conflict, blame, aggressive behavior, and an environment that is sorely lacking in support.

Ultimately, gossip and blame will create a blockage of energy, and engagement needs a clear flow of energy in order to function well. We can compare this to feng shui. In the practice of feng shui, you want to create a positive flow of energy by removing blockages or obstacles in a given room. If there are clunky objects or even if something is simply positioned wrong, it can throw off the energetic balance of a space. The same is true in any workplace. If a team member is conveying frustration and uncertainty to those around them, this can block engagement and motivation. Therefore, it's important to clear the blockage by opening a dialogue with the team member and solving any issues or concerns they have. Once they feel that they have more clarity and support, engagement will begin to flow once again.

How to Use Your Body Language and Micro Expressions to Be Congruent with Engagement

When it comes to body language and micro expressions, the most important thing to consider is your energy. Engagement requires an active energy, and the way you move and interact with others should reflect this.

ACTIVE ENERGY

If you've ever watched Steve Jobs on stage, you've likely noticed that he engaged the audience by walking around, gesticulating with his hands to emphasize points, varying his tone, and so on. While that kind of style works great during a presentation, it's not necessary to go that far when speaking one-on-one or even to a small team. The idea is to offer a vibrant energy that others can feed off of.

We all have days when we are feeling sluggish or unmotivated. When that happens, pay attention to the times when you need to communicate with your employees. If you are able to offer a few minutes of active energy to the conversation, you will be able to increase both your engagement and theirs.

You can think of your energy like the rhythm of a song. There are probably several songs that will automatically cause you to sway side to side, tap your fingers to the beat, or even dance spontaneously. Music can influence how you move and feel. The same is true for the energy you exude. Active, positive energy will cause those around you to engage more with what you're doing and saying, while sluggish, negative energy will do the opposite. Paying attention to the tempo and tone of your speech, as well as to the way you move your body, can create a rhythm of engagement that others will be able to get on board with.

ENGAGED BODY LANGUAGE

There are many ways you can use your body language to enhance engagement. When speaking to others, use open gestures, as this will demonstrate mental openness. Use your hands to underscore important points. Smile, make eye contact, and nod to demonstrate that you're listening. When you ask a question, lead forward and engage in active listening. This means that if you are doing another activity, step away from it so that you can be fully present in what the other person is saying. When you do this, you will demonstrate curiosity and interest, which naturally enhance engagement.

Review this table to learn more about which gestures and micro expressions support engagement and which block engagement:

BODY LANGUAGE AND MICRO EXPRESSIONS THAT SUPPORT ENGAGEMENT	BODY LANGUAGE AND MICRO EXPRESSIONS THAT BLOCK ENGAGEMENT
• Smiling with muscles around the eye contracted, showing wrinkles	• Frowning or shaking head
• Nodding	• Eye rolling or excessive blinking
• Making eye contact	• Pointing with finger (suggests aggression)
• Drawing with hands	• Body faces away from the other person
• Body faces the other person	• Pressed lips
• Relaxed shoulders	• Crossed arms or legs
• Open hands, especially when wrists are shown	• Tapping foot or hands
• Wide, confident stance	• The movement of hiding behind an object (such as a laptop)

BODY LANGUAGE AND MICRO EXPRESSIONS THAT SUPPORT ENGAGEMENT (CONT.)	BODY LANGUAGE AND MICRO EXPRESSIONS THAT BLOCK ENGAGEMENT (CONT.)
• Upper eyelids raised in surprise	• Uneven smile with only one lip corner up (a micro expression of contempt)
• Contempt with one lip corner raised, timed so as to indicate pride	• Contempt with only one lip corner raised, timed so as to indicate superiority
• Happiness expression with both lip corners up	• Brows lowered and/or eyelids tightened in anger

How to Identify Engagement in Body Language and Micro Expressions Using the BLINK Technique

In situations where you want to gauge the level of engagement in your employees or team members using the BLINK technique, it's important to avoid open-ended questions, as those questions make it easy to answer in an indirect or deceptive way. That can make it difficult to receive useful information from the body language and micro expressions of the speaker.

Instead, you can effectively use the BLINK technique by stating different options. To offer an example related to engagement, imagine a manager speaking to a team member about their potential to bring new customers to their company. The customers must match a certain profile to fit with the company's goals.

The first scenario the leader presents may sound something like this: "I know some of our colleagues would be happy to participate in this new task because finding new customers is a great opportunity to discover new possibilities and potential for our sales. This could bring a lot of success to our company, and if we do things right, we can have ten new customers per week, which will bring in money for our future initiatives."

Note that in this scenario, the leader isn't using "you" to speak specifically about the team member they're conversing with. This helps the team member avoid feeling judged or put on the spot. When using the BLINK technique, it's often more effective to speak about a hypothetical third party. In the example, that third party is "our colleagues," but it could be even more general, such as "people."

How does the person respond to the stated scenario? Do they smile and nod? Do they lean forward as if engaged and interested in what you're saying? Do they begin to turn their body away or shift from one foot to the other? Note their reaction and whether it seems to be positive or negative.

The next step to gauge their engagement with a potential task would be to present a scenario that indicates resistance. For example: "I know that sometimes when our colleagues are facing a new task or situation, they may feel nervous about looking for new customers, which can be a difficult task when you don't have good connections. This kind of task can involve a lot of cold calls and failed efforts, so people might experience rejection when they start a new initiative like this. It's possible that it will take a great deal of time and effort to bring customers to this sector."

Now, how does the person respond to this scenario as you're speaking? Do they look down or make more eye contact? Do they cross their arms or open their stance? Check the positive or negative energy associated with their reaction.

Here, since we're talking about engagement, it's important to end on a positive note and not leave your team member or employee with the negative scenario. For example, after the final scenario, you could say, "Luckily, that's not the case in our company because many people want to collaborate with us, so I'm sure there are lots of new clients who want to partner up." By ending with a sense of optimism, you can avoid any decrease in motivation or engagement.

If you notice that your team member seemed to relate more to the negative scenario, tap into empathy to discuss their reasons for not feeling engaged with the hypothetical task you want to give them. You may find that they offer feedback that can bring fresh new ideas to the project, so this may also be a good time to refer back to chapter 1, Adaptability, as the situation may call for a change.

●

Integrating Engagement into Who You Are

When you wake up in the morning, how do you feel about the day ahead of you and about life in general? Do you want to wake up and get out of bed to start your day? Do you want to pull the covers over your head and stay in bed for a few more hours? However you answered, it's important to understand why.

Integrating engagement into who you are on a daily basis has a great deal to do with the kind of energy you cultivate. If you tend to wake up with a lot of energy and feel good about starting the day, you're off to a good start. If you wake up with low energy and a sluggish demeanor, it may be time to look into some strategies to cultivate more positive, active energy. Here are some strategies to uplift your mood and increase engagement.

GRATITUDE MEDITATION

The moment you wake up is the moment in your day with the most potential. This is the time when you can infuse positive or negative energy into how you go through the rest of your day. What can help a great deal is taking those first moments to meditate and breathe deeply for, say, just ten minutes.

During those ten minutes, take time to appreciate all of the positive things in your life. Cultivate gratitude for your family, your house, your job, the food in your cabinet, and more, all while breathing deeply to spread relaxation throughout your body.

Research in the area of positive psychology has shown that experiencing and expressing gratitude can increase optimism and well-being, which can be powerful tools as you seek to grow your sense of engagement in life. Set your alarm ten minutes early so that you don't feel rushed during your morning routine, and try your own gratitude meditation to start your day on a positive note.

POSITIVE STRESS EXPERIENCE

I know you don't want to start your day with any kind of stress, but a positive stress experience is simply a way to trigger a sense of alertness and awareness. In this case, I suggest a hot and cold shower. Right after waking, step into the shower and alternate between hot and cold water. This can help you boost your energy and eliminate any sluggishness.

In the past, people would use a container of cold water from the closest water source to throw water on their faces in the morning as a way to wake themselves up. If you don't yet feel ready to take on a hot-cold shower, try splashing cold water on your face, which can have a similar effect.

ADDING MOTIVATIONAL NOTES TO YOUR ENVIRONMENT

Motivational notes can take the form of uplifting music for some. For others, it might mean putting an inspiring quote on their nightstand to read the moment they wake up. You can also set an inspiring book on your nightstand to pick up for just a few minutes after waking. Anything you find motivational or inspirational can help shift your mood in a positive direction and get your day started in a way that will naturally enhance your engagement.

• • •

While there are many things you can do to increase your energy in the morning, there are some things you should avoid doing, as they can cultivate negative energy and decrease motivation.

AVOID LISTENING TO THE NEWS

Listening to the news first thing in the morning can put a damper on your energy. Most of the news we hear tends to be very negative and can push us into a depressive mood. This is part of mental hygiene. Just as you want to keep your body clean, you should also keep your mind clean, at least for the first few vulnerable moments of your day. During that time, you are still moving from the delta and alpha state to the beta state, which means you are primed to engage in self-healing. This is the time to inhibit negative thoughts, anxiety, and depression and to focus on uplifting, healing activities.

AVOID CHECKING EMAILS

For many people, emails are a necessary part of their job and life. But they don't have to encroach on your day first thing in the morning. If you know that you will likely encounter challenging or negative emails when you open your inbox, put it to the side during the first hour of your day. There will be time to respond to all of your emails later.

HAPPINESS IS CONSTANT

Research has shown that people tend to maintain the same level of happiness throughout their life, independent of their circumstances. This is known as the hedonic treadmill. That's why there's no better time than now to work on improving your baseline level of well-being and sense of engagement with life.

The start of your day is crucial in your attempts to increase your overall engagement. Use that time to check in with how you feel, where your thoughts go, and the type of energy you're cultivating. Planning the first thirty minutes of your day to include uplifting activities and shifting your attention toward the positive things in life can do wonders for your engagement.

Helping Others Integrate Engagement into Their Lives

As I mentioned earlier in the chapter, engagement revolves around a vibrant, active energy. You likely know someone who, as soon as they walk into a room, can shift the energy in a positive direction. As a leader, you can do the same for your team members and employees.

CHANGE THE ENVIRONMENT

Changing the environment that your team members are working in is a good way to shift the dynamic. For example, imagine working in an office with low lighting, closed blinds, and grayscale walls. That doesn't sound like an environment that promotes engagement. Simply adding some extra lighting or allowing employees to open their windows can do a great deal to help them be more active and engaged with what they're doing.

If you see someone who is in a particularly sluggish or negative space, you may need to temporarily remove them from the environment entirely. That can be as simple as taking them out to lunch or moving their office to another part of the building.

HELP THE ENERGY FLOW

Referring back to the example of feng shui, remember that energy cannot flow when there are blockages. The same is true for the energy of your team. If you see two coworkers who constantly disagree and fail to complete projects when working together, it may be time to consider separating them, as their negative energy could be causing a blockage within the entire team. If they are two people who must work together, you can consider a coach to bring them together and help them understand how they can work together more effectively.

DEMONSTRATE YOUR OWN SENSE OF ENGAGEMENT

If you notice that engagement is a problem within your team, try bringing everyone into a single space where you are also working. As they work near you, you can demonstrate how you stay engaged with the task in front of you. As I mentioned before, through your own rhythm of engagement, you can bring people in so that they begin to move to the same beat.

When I had employees at my training company, I would often work alone, but there were times when I would work with my employees in the same space. I noticed that this helped them be more engaged, as their sense of teamwork increased. I was also able to feel out the energy around certain projects and get clued in to any gossip that was floating around. I was then able to use empathy to address any problems and use my own engagement to engage others.

CHAPTER FOUR

TRANSPARENCY

● ● ● ● ● ● ● ●

Being transparent as a leader is about building trust. When people around you feel that you are giving them all of the information, they will trust what you say, and they will trust that nothing is being hidden. If a lack of transparency is the status quo, it can breed gossip and conspiracy theories. Leaving room for rumors to spread is a sure way to decrease trust and increase friction within a company or team.

Sharing details about resources, strategies, and processes can help your team members understand not only why certain things are happening but what their role looks like and how it may develop. Presenting everyone with all the available information can shut down negative opinions based in gossip. Those kinds of negative opinions are much harder to manage than critiques of specific information that is given.

MORE INFORMATION LEADS TO MORE TRUST

Good (and bad) examples of transparency can be found in the clothing industry, specifically in how they approach sustainability. ARKET (arket.com) is one such company that does its best to be transparent about where its materials come from and how they are produced. If you go to their website, you will find a grid where you can explore everything from the source of their materials, their suppliers, and their environmental impact. After you have visited their site, you will likely feel that you know exactly who they are, what their goals are, and what you are getting when you buy a piece of clothing from them. You would be hard-pressed to find something to negatively critique, and it would be even more difficult to find space to create doubt about what they are doing as a company.

Many other clothing companies fail to list their materials and where they come from, or they provide vague or misleading information because they believe that hiding that information is safer than making it public. Not only does this sow distrust, but it leaves a lot of space for customers to assume that unethical practices are taking place, whether that is true or not. It also suggests that the company itself is not proud or comfortable with what it is doing, which does little to convince a potential customer to buy something from them.

The same is true for any leader. Even if there are things you would prefer not to share, offering that information to your team members will help them feel that you are being truthful with them, and they will likely feel that they are able to relate to you more. If they feel that you are hiding information from them, they will feel uneasy or suspicious, which can create tension between you and your team, as well as between team members themselves, as gossip begins to spread.

SHORT-TERM AND LONG-TERM CONSEQUENCES

While hiding inconvenient information can be good for short-term sales or growth, in the long term, it will undermine the reputation of a company and its leaders. Dealing with negative opinions related to a temporary situation that you share with everyone is much easier than dealing with constant negative opinions that grow from a lack of information. In the end, building a space where gossip, rumors, and conspiracy theories can thrive is counterproductive for the external image, reputation, and functionality of a company or leader.

How to Recognize Transparency in Yourself and Others

Transparency involves self-reflection. For many, it seems obvious that you are transparent and are sharing all of the relevant information with those who are on your team. You may believe that the way you work makes it obvious what others should know. But it's likely not obvious, as your team members will come from different backgrounds, cultures, or companies, which can alter their perspectives. While you believe you are making information clear, the way they process what you present to them may not bring them to the conclusions you had assumed would be obvious.

For that reason, you should practice being explicit with the information you offer, in order to avoid any misunderstandings. Fortunately, transparency *is* something that can be practiced and learned. As a leader, it's important to express your plans, goals, vision, and mission, as well as to explain your reasoning behind each of those. When you are transparent with this information, people will be more willing to help and support you.

Think of a puzzle with many pieces. When you finish the puzzle, you notice that three spaces are still empty—you're missing three puzzle pieces. The natural tendency of your mind is to imagine what those three pieces look like in order to create a mental image of the completed puzzle. The same happens with gaps in information. If a leader fails to be transparent and leaves space for individual interpretations or assumptions, people will fill in the missing information with their imaginations. At this point, you, as a leader, lose control of the narrative, and distrust starts to grow. Instead, it's best to complete the mental puzzle for your team members so that they have all the information they need.

How can you tell if you're being fully transparent and offering all the puzzle pieces that your team needs?

HOW MUCH YOU SHARE

To discover whether you are being transparent, check how much you are really sharing with those around you. When describing your plan for the next six months, do you offer an overview, or do you go through step-by-step to provide complete clarity?

It's also important to discover how you feel when you share information. When you share your six-month plan, do you feel confident and comfortable, or do you experience unease and nervousness? If sharing more information causes you discomfort, you may be struggling with transparency.

If you tend to hide things and share information only once a project has been successfully completed, this can suggest a lack of confidence, but it also indicates that your transparency is quite low. However, if you bring your team in at the start of a project and share your plan, goals, and expectations, as well as answer any questions your team asks, this indicates a higher comfort level with transparency.

HOW TRANSPARENCY AFFECTS COLLABORATION

You've likely met employees or coworkers who prefer to work alone. They share few details about their ongoing projects, don't ask many questions, and only ask for feedback when it becomes impossible to move forward without it. On the other hand, there are those who go to leadership with detailed plans and ask for feedback and suggestions. You can probably see which one is considered more transparent. It should also be obvious which one is easier to work with. It is much easier to collaborate with someone who is comfortable being transparent.

When it comes to collaboration, it can be important to take the time to train your team members how to be more transparent, as this will improve teamwork overall. To do this, ask them to prepare a plan, reason through how they want to proceed, and create discussions around problems that could arise. This will build trust, but it will also help them practice transparency and get comfortable with sharing information.

When we are able to share with those around us, it's easier to receive input and support and to feel that you aren't alone. In the world today, many people work long hours and put in those long hours without interacting with others. We do not share what we do because nobody asks about it. If you, as a leader, create transparency within your team, you can reduce individuals' sense of isolation and improve efficiency, as sharing will benefit the development of plans and open space for feedback and discussions.

PERSONAL SHARING

While I've focused on transparency around work tasks and projects up to this point, it's also important to talk about transparency on a personal level. Sharing private details about our lives is not always necessary or appropriate, but there are times where it can create greater understanding and team cohesion.

For example, if you know there are things in your personal life that could affect your team members or employees, such as views on religion, politics, or general attitudes toward work and life, it would be a good idea to be transparent about those things. Consider a team member who is vegetarian. If they were not transparent about their diet, you could put them in an uncomfortable position by taking everyone out to a barbecue restaurant one day. Wouldn't it have been better to have avoided the awkward situation altogether by being open about this detail?

I was once delivering a training session in Qatar. We decided to discuss religion among the participants beforehand, and it ended up helping us deliver a more effective presentation. We discovered that some of the videos we had planned to show weren't appropriate for the beliefs of many of the training participants, as the videos weren't aligned with the views of Islam. In this case, we also had to be transparent about our stereotypes and discuss what we had assumed would be appropriate and what wouldn't. By being transparent about these personal details, we were able to create a space where everyone felt respected.

The bottom line is that it's best to avoid making assumptions and to use transparency to be sure. Otherwise, the hidden information will leak through your body language and micro expressions, cluing others into the fact that transparency is not being practiced.

| 1 | 2 | 3 | 4 | 5 | 6 | 7 | 8 | 9 | 10 |

$\longleftrightarrow$

LOW TRANSPARENCY   **HIGH TRANSPARENCY**

This is a scale you can use to measure the transparency of each member of your team and then discuss what may need to be improved.

How to Verbally Communicate Transparency

Verbally communicating transparency goes beyond what you say and includes how you say it. It starts with the kind of language you use when talking with individuals. For example, if you are a lawyer trying to explain an upcoming case to your colleagues, you will be able to use more legal vocabulary, as they will understand it. If you want to be clear and transparent with your client, however, you will have to scale back the legal vocabulary, as they likely won't understand it, and information could get lost or be misinterpreted.

Communicating in a way that others can understand is key. If you aren't sure if you're being entirely clear or transparent, a simple exercise you can practice is to ask the other person to summarize what you've just said. This is generally most helpful when the information you're giving them is very important and something that needs to be understood in order for both parties to move forward.

COMMUNICATING TRANSPARENCY WITH PERSONAL INFORMATION

While it's important to know what and how much information you want to share with someone when it comes to personal matters, it's also important to choose the right moment to share it. Sharing information about your religion, political interests, ideology, or beliefs will likely feel important to you, but others may not understand that they should take it seriously. To make sure the moment is right for them to receive the information you're offering, ask them directly to pay attention to what you're about to say. You can say, for example, "I would like to share some personal information with you. Do you have a few minutes to speak with me?" Through this simple statement and question, you can prepare them to be an active listener and reduce distractions.

Transparency is about communicating things that help others understand you, support you, or collaborate with you. Being transparent and sharing information takes time and effort, so make sure you are being taken seriously when the moment arises.

OVERSHARING

When people learn the importance of transparency, they can develop the tendency to overshare. They begin to include details about plans that aren't important for the team, or they focus on areas that could be left for a later time. Offering too much information can overwhelm a listener and make it difficult for them to know what the takeaway of a conversation should be.

In this case, it's crucial to understand what information your listener needs from you and what is enough information to help them move forward. To make sure this goal is being achieved, I suggest asking questions like, "Is there more information that you would like to know about this?" or "Do you have any questions about what we've just spoken about?" Offering them the space to request more information can help you learn what your team members need and expect from you.

YOU DON'T HAVE TO EXPLAIN YOURSELF

Marshall Goldsmith has consistently been an excellent example of someone in my life who practices transparency. When I speak to him or ask him questions, he answers in an honest, direct way. While he is always transparent with the information he gives, he doesn't ever feel the need to explain himself or make excuses for the plans or actions he presents. He approaches all conversations with a sense of certainty and honesty.

For example, when I was preparing to film him for *The Earned Life*, he stated that he always wears a green shirt and khaki pants, so that's what he wanted to be filmed wearing. While this may seem like a strange habit to some, Marshall didn't feel the need to explain himself or feel embarrassed about his clothing choices. Nor did he need to. No one was blaming him for his choices, so there was no need to make excuses. He was confident in his decision, so I felt comfortable with it as well.

When you begin to explain yourself unnecessarily, it can suggest a lack of confidence or insecurity in your plans, opinions, or ideas. As a leader, you don't want your team members to feel uncomfortable with the information you're offering them. The best way to avoid that is to share information in a way that is clear and direct and that leaves as little space for misunderstanding as possible. If you practice transparency in an honest way, people will often accept it and respect it.

RECOGNIZING TRANSPARENCY IN OTHERS

To determine how transparent others are, pay attention to the details they share. Do they often talk about their past accomplishments but leave out information about their past failures? Do they overexaggerate wins but gloss over losses? Even if they share a great deal about one part of their experience, if they leave out all of the other parts, this may indicate a lack of transparency.

It's important to note that some people simply aren't accustomed to transparent language, so while they may not approach you to share information, they may be very willing to answer questions when asked. This is less a lack of transparency and more a lack of awareness about what they should or could be sharing. In that case, it may just take them time to get used to being open and honest with their thoughts and ideas.

How to Use Your Body Language and Micro Expressions to Be Congruent with Transparency

The attitude you bring to the information you are sharing is key in transparency. If you decide to hide information, it will inevitably come through in your body language and micro expressions.

Consider Bill Clinton's false statement about his relationship with Monica Lewinsky: "I did not have sexual relations with that woman, Miss Lewinsky." I was asked to analyze that moment in his speech during my training, and it was interesting to note that there was no obviously negative body language suggesting a lie, but there was also no body language indicating authenticity. The other parts of his speech were given in a natural tone of voice, but when this statement arose, it was given in a more robotic tone, and he began to use his hands to match the rhythm of the statement. These were indications that the statement had been practiced, which is why it was lacking signs of honesty and transparency.

The lesson here is that even if you master hiding negative body language, that doesn't mean that you have mastered the art of appearing authentic. If you are trying to pressure your body to be congruent with untruths, it will require a great deal of focus, and doing it well is tricky, even for skillful leaders. In the long term, it's easier and more productive to learn to share difficult truths with those who know you, as they will likely learn to pick up signals that you aren't being completely transparent.

Review this table to learn more about which gestures and micro expressions support engagement and which block engagement:

BODY LANGUAGE AND MICRO EXPRESSIONS THAT INDICATE TRANSPARENCY	BODY LANGUAGE AND MICRO EXPRESSIONS THAT SUGGEST A LACK OF TRANSPARENCY
• Open smile	• Scratching head
• Relaxed shoulders	• Touching nose
• Open hands	• Placing body behind objects or furniture
• Matching and congruent micro expressions to what is said	• Contradictory micro expressions that do not match what is said

The most important takeaway from this table is that relaxation is a strong indicator of transparency, as stress can indicate that there's something going on that you don't want people to know. Furthermore, stress and dishonesty often present in very similar ways when it comes to body language. While there may be some other cause of the stress, those you are speaking with will tend to connect stress with a lack of honesty. Therefore, as a leader, it's important to work on your well-being through relaxation and breathing techniques in order to support your transparency.

How to Recognize Transparency in Body Language and Micro Expressions Using the BLINK Technique

Observing transparency involves checking in to see how honest people are with the information they offer. Using the BLINK technique, you want to offer various options that relate to something you have recently spoken to a team member about. For example, consider that you have doubts about whether a team member is attending all of the meetings that they say they are attending. They may not want to share that they are skipping some meetings because they feel too busy, tired, or uninterested. But they likely won't share that information with you, as they may fear backlash. In this case, BLINK can be a helpful technique.

For the first scenario you present, you can say something like: "Many of the sales professionals are attending all the meetings, and they're very good about being on time, taking good notes, and offering interesting insights. It seems very helpful for their work."

As another option, you can say: "Other sales professionals here are skipping meetings because they don't believe it has value for them. They think the meetings are boring or don't relate to their role here, so they prefer to spend time with customers in the field."

A final option could be: "Other sales professionals are attending certain meetings and skipping others because they are overwhelmed with work and find the meetings too demanding."

By presenting these three situations, you can see how the listener reacts, as well as the micro expressions they show. Do they look away or cross their arms when you talk about the team members who are skipping meetings? Do they smile when you talk about those who are attending each meeting diligently? Observe their reactions to see which option resonates most with them.

MAKE IT RELATABLE

When creating the options for the BLINK technique here, it's important to put yourself in the listener's shoes. Create options that are aligned with the reality they live every day, as well as the attitudes you've been observing at the company.

By making the options relatable and realistic, you can gain valuable insight into what people are doing and how they may be thinking about different parts of their work. Keep in mind, however, that these insights shouldn't be used to judge or confront a team member. The BLINK technique is simply a way to create more understanding within your team so that you can be more effective as a leader.

Integrating Transparency into Who You Are

As with any change you are trying to make, it's good to start small in order to practice and create new habits. When it comes to transparency, you can try opening up about small daily occurrences that you would usually keep to yourself in order to learn how people react. You will likely find that hearing those kinds of things is not such a big deal for others. You may also realize that being transparent makes overall communication easier because each side knows how to react to what's being shared.

HOW TRANSPARENCY SHAPES RELATIONSHIPS

There is a well-known story about a husband and a wife eating breakfast together. Every day for twenty years they had eaten burger buns with their breakfast. The husband always ate the top of the bun, while the wife always ate the bottom. Each of them assumed that the other preferred the piece that they always took. After twenty years, they accidentally realized that each preferred the opposite piece. From then on, they were each more content at breakfast because they were finally eating the piece of the bun that they wanted.

This is a simple but telling example of how transparency can shift your relationship with others. Often, we keep information to ourselves because we believe it may hurt someone else. What the story demonstrates is that you never really know, and keeping information to yourself may unintentionally create resentment that can grow over time.

A lack of transparency in any personal or professional relationship can cause tension, frustration, and unhappiness. Knowing the preferences of each side can open up larger conversations that benefit both parties and make it easier to communicate. For the husband and wife in the story, their small realization about the bun likely opened up other conversations that led to greater understanding and happiness.

PRACTICING TRANSPARENCY

When entering situations that involve new people or other cultures, it can feel uncomfortable to share your personal preferences or beliefs. But these are some of the best moments to practice transparency!

I traveled to Siberia some years ago to have meetings with local people. I knew before I went that people in that area enjoy drinking hard alcohol and eating meat, two things that I wasn't comfortable with at the time. Instead of allowing it to cause an uncomfortable situation, I told everyone up front that I preferred not to drink hard alcohol or eat meat. Instead of being offended at my choice, those that I was meeting with were happy to accommodate me and help me feel comfortable. At our first dinner together, I was offered a plate of fish and a beer while the others ate meat and drank vodka. We were all happy with what we had in front of us, and we were able to talk and share experiences and enjoy the time together.

Over the years, I have discovered that people want to please you. In general, no one enjoys embarrassment or having to guess when information is unknown. We prefer to be able to make a plan or be aware of information ahead of time in order to prepare ourselves and to find common ground with those around us. That is only possible when transparency is being practiced.

Helping Others Integrate Transparency into Their Lives

CREATING THE RIGHT ATMOSPHERE

Creating an atmosphere of openness and honesty is key if you want to encourage others to be more transparent. As a leader, you are a role model, so if you are reserved and judgmental toward others, this will set a precedent that others will follow. If instead you share your opinions and ideas and encourage others to do the same, everyone will feel that they are in a space where it is safe and where they can be transparent without backlash.

AVOID EXCLUSION

One of the enemies of transparency is exclusion. I have worked with companies where I have seen that there are individual circles that purposely exclude some people. They may exclude them based on personality or skill set or some other criteria, but the thing that matters is that people are being excluded at all. If the circles close up too much and exclude too many people, the company can become divided. In this case, transparency is often lost because there are too many secrets and not enough sharing.

On our film sets, we always make sure to have meetings where everyone is present. There may be information that is more helpful for some than for others, but in the end everyone feels included and can understand what is going on. This creates more cohesion and offers a space where everyone can share their thoughts on upcoming plans.

●

Making Space for Sharing

IN YOUR PRIVATE LIFE

Nowadays, it's easy to feel that we are sharing enough because we often post pictures and updates on social media. This makes it difficult to remember to share with those we interact with face-to-face, including our friends and family. Ultimately, we end up feeling isolated and unfulfilled because we have closed the spaces where we used to share our struggles, accomplishments, thoughts, and emotions.

A good place to re-create a space for sharing is around the dinner table. Dinnertime is ideal, as everyone comes together and is ready to relax after what may have been a trying or long day. This can be a time to ask everyone to put their phones away and share something about their day. It may happen that someone isn't used to practicing transparency and may be reluctant to share. In that case, you can try actively asking questions to help them open up and learn that they are in a safe space.

AT WORK

The same can be done at your workplace. One good example is casual Fridays. While this doesn't work for all companies, it's a good example, as it shows what can happen when you create a more relaxed atmosphere, even if it's just one day a week. Creating a space where people feel more open and able to be themselves can help them share more information about themselves or what they have been experiencing at work. This can be very positive for your workplace as a whole, as it will help your team members feel heard and more committed to the goals and mission of the company.

PART 2
INNER SKILLS

CHAPTER FIVE

COURAGE

● ● ● ● ● ● ●

Nelson Mandela, Martin Luther King Jr., Mahatma Gandhi. Everyone has heard of these great leaders, people who altered the course of history through their actions. These leaders demonstrated a great deal of courage through their goals, but being courageous does not have to mean changing an entire country's ideology.

Courage can be shown on a smaller scale by sharing honest thoughts and promoting positive changes at a company or within a team. The world needs more people who are willing to stand up for the values and for what they believe to be right. Being complacent is easier than being courageous, but complacency rarely leads to honest, positive change.

THE IMPORTANCE OF FINDING YOUR TRIBE

While it can often feel that those who are courageous leaders must act alone as they stand up against a force larger than themselves, this has rarely been true. Even great leaders like Nelson Mandela and Martin Luther King Jr. had friends and allies who helped promote their vision of a better future.

As a leader seeking to practice courage and work toward positive change, it's best to begin by building your tribe. These are people who understand and support your philosophy, values, and actions. If you work to create a group of like-minded people, this helps you as you move forward with your goals. Fortunately, finding your tribe nowadays is significantly easier, as we have access to social media, networking spaces, and online communication where we can share our ideas more freely with others.

START WITH SMALL, COURAGEOUS ACTIONS

If you are a leader in a corporation, you probably understand that you need to work within the confines of your company's policies or risk getting fired. In those cases, it can be difficult to be courageous and move away from the norm. That's why it can be more effective to start with small steps.

For example, you can start by talking to your coworkers or team members to get their thoughts and feedback on various aspects of the workplace. If you see room for improvement, such as in new practices or ethical codes you want to build into the company, start slowly by developing your logic and reasoning behind this. It's impossible to revolutionize a company overnight, and while you may not make it into the history books of the future, you can still affect your space in a positive way.

KAIZEN

Kaizen is a Japanese philosophy that suggests that improvement can come through small, ongoing, positive changes. Toyota uses this philosophy to encourage individual employees to suggest areas of improvement and possible solutions.

You can think of *kaizen* in terms of writing a book. If you try to write a complete book overnight, you will likely fail. But if you approach the book one word, sentence, or chapter at a time, your odds of success go up as you make continuous progress.

CHARISMA AND COURAGE

One important element of courage is how you communicate your message. It's significantly easier to share important messages that people will listen to if you use charisma, demonstrate confidence, and back up your ideas with examples and reasoning. Charisma can help you build momentum by drawing people into your ideas and capturing their attention.

It's important to note that charisma won't get you very far if you choose the wrong moment to share your message. If the information is something that you hope will change your company or possibly take people by surprise, it's important to find a good moment when everyone is able to pay attention and have time to consider your words. It may not be a good idea, for example, to speak about such things around the table at a team luncheon.

I had a chance to practice this myself when I was fifteen and spending time at a winter camp. There was a small group of girls who were not fond of one of my friends, and they began to spread a rumor that she had robbed money from another girl. I checked the room and saw that they had tried to put money in her pack. I had to choose an appropriate moment to approach the director of the camp to try to convince her not to expel my friend. I took the time to calmly convince her what I believe had happened and why my friend deserved to remain at the camp. I did my best to speak clearly and charismatically while also presenting reasoning and evidence to support my ideas.

And it helped. My friend wasn't expelled, and the situation was sorted out, with apologies offered on all sides. For the rest of camp, she didn't experience any more bullying or rumors. In this case, courage was required, as there were things that needed to be stated loudly and clearly.

It can often happen that similar, unethical practices come up at companies, and it's important to bring those things to light and share your opinion, independent of the possible outcome. While many leaders fear backlash from speaking up in this way, it usually will not result in the person getting fired, as that would demonstrate guilt and culpability from the superiors.

●

How to Recognize Courage in Yourself and Others

Courage is about fearlessness. It's about being in a position where you no longer care to stay inside your comfort zone. Whether it's small or big, you decide that the time has come to find a way through or to push for a change, despite the fact that it may bring you discomfort or difficulties. There is a kind of energy that develops before courage, an energy that pushes you to say something out loud or take action when you know you should.

MEASURING YOUR LEVEL OF COURAGE

As with many traits, it's possible to give yourself a kind of score on your level of courage. You can do this by looking at how you approach various situations in your daily life. For example, imagine you are at a restaurant and receive a dirty spoon. In this case, would you ask the waiter for a new one or simply use the dirty spoon to avoid any discomfort? The former would increase your courage score, while the latter would lower it.

There could be more complicated situations in which you have to decide whether you will stand up to or offer your opinion to someone in a position of authority. Consider a situation where you disagree with a decision your boss has made. Would you go to them and present your position and respectfully let them know why you disagree? Or would you keep your thoughts to yourself and allow the decision to stand without protest?

WHEN IT'S EASIER TO BE COURAGEOUS

You don't have to tackle huge changes like Martin Luther King Jr. to be courageous. Acting courageously in small, daily situations is just as important. If you stand up for yourself, express your opinions, and ask companies to improve their service when necessary, you can help make small, beneficial changes in the world around you. But this can be difficult for some personalities.

For example, if you are naturally shy, courage may not come as easily to you. You may prefer to wait until after you leave the restaurant to write an email to the company voicing your unhappiness. Or you may prefer to keep your opinions to yourself.

Courage can also be more difficult for people of a certain gender, age, or ethnicity. A Caucasian man in his forties, for example, will likely be more at ease sharing his opinions than a Caucasian woman in her twenties due to the differing values societies place on men and women.

With that said, you can practice being courageous at any time, despite your gender, age, or ethnicity, and it's important to do so.

When I was in my twenties, I started my first company as a young woman in Poland. It wasn't very common at the time to start a business so young, let alone as a woman. I was often in positions where I would need to speak with middle-aged men to negotiate deals related to the training I was offering. I realized at the time that I had two options. I could act in the way everyone expected me to act as a woman by being reserved and unsure, or I could work to move beyond those limiting beliefs to grow my reputation. By representing who I was and what I wanted to achieve with my business, I was able to close many deals regardless of people's first impressions of me. Body language, charisma, and preparation were key to helping me succeed, and they are important factors as you work to practice courage.

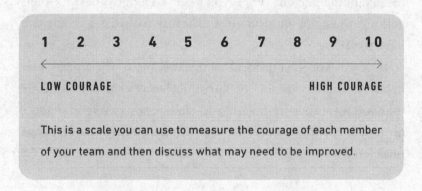

This is a scale you can use to measure the courage of each member of your team and then discuss what may need to be improved.

How to Verbally Communicate Courage

When trying to communicate with courage, it's important to find the right moment to speak. You want to find a time when those you are speaking with can offer their complete attention without being distracted by other tasks, devices, or conversations. If you are speaking about an important situation that you want to change, you want everyone to be able to focus on what you are trying to convey.

DESCRIBE THE BEHAVIOR

Using courage to change situations is a worthy pursuit, but the way you approach the conversations you need to have can have a huge effect on how those conversations go. When speaking to others about a problem you want to solve or a behavior you want to change, it's key to address it by describing the behavior instead of the person. When you begin to judge others for their actions, they can shut down and refuse to listen to what you have to say.

Instead, express your ideas using facts about why a particular behavior is unacceptable or harmful. Do your best to indicate that you want to work together to change something and agree on new behaviors or actions that are acceptable for everyone involved.

GIVE OTHERS THE BENEFIT OF THE DOUBT

As you address problems with individuals' behavior, it's always good to assume that they weren't purposely trying to cause harm. If, for example, they were bullying a coworker, it's better to approach them with the understanding that they may not have realized that the way they were treating that coworker was hurtful. This can help to avoid triggering defensiveness and to open pathways to change and collaboration.

Of course, there are some behaviors that are entirely unacceptable and without remedy, and those need to be approached in a completely different way. But if the behavior seems to be something that can be improved or turned around, approach it as a mistake that can be learned from as opposed to a personality flaw that is permanent.

MANAGING ANGER

Make sure you analyze your motivations before speaking up. Are you trying to change a situation because you've looked at it from all angles and have concluded that it would be better for the team if it changed? Or are you simply angry about a particular situation and feel the need to vent your frustrations to clear your head?

It's good to check in with your level of anger to ensure you don't inadvertently say things that could be considered harmful or judgmental. Approaching any situation with a relaxed, confident demeanor can do wonders for the outcome, as it can encourage others in the conversation to also relax and settle into a more rational state of mind.

Once you have relaxed, you will be able to communicate without aggression and without demonstrating too much emotion. Lean into facts and descriptions of behaviors you want to change, as this will help others enter the conversation more rationally as well. If you start to use emotional words, you can trigger the limbic system of those listening, which could cause them to become angry or defensive. For that reason, it's better to steer the conversation using more rational arguments, as opposed to more emotional ones.

How to Notice if Others Are Verbally Communicating Courage

Recognizing courage in others can be tricky, as what feels courageous to one person may not seem courageous to another. For example, if someone is shy, it will take more effort to communicate something that they feel is important or alarming. They may be afraid to speak up or feel nervous, which could cause them to pick the wrong moment to speak with someone or to share information in a way that feels disjointed or incoherent.

Technically speaking, those people may not be very courageous in the way they are communicating, but for them, the act of simply speaking up in any way may be a courageous act, especially if they are at a lower position in the company hierarchy. For that reason, it's important to always recognize their effort when they come to you with a concern, and engage in active listening to hear them out.

HOW CULTURE AFFECTS COURAGE

People from certain cultures may have difficulty sharing things they consider to be negative or problematic. For example, people who grew up in some Asian cultures may be more reserved with this kind of information and reluctant to discuss problems, especially with those who are not from the same culture. You may notice that they try to work in small conversations related to the problem in an otherwise relaxed, normal conversation. In these cases, it's important to pick up on the fact that they want to share something and help them to be courageous by opening a space where they can feel safer discussing it.

ACKNOWLEDGE COURAGE

There are some people for whom courage comes quite naturally, and they are often able to speak up and present information around things they would like to change. It can be easy to overlook these people, as they seem so comfortable with what they are saying. But in these cases, as a leader, it's important to acknowledge and thank them for speaking up and bringing the problem to your attention. Whether someone is naturally courageous or not, it can still be difficult to mentally prepare yourself for difficult discussions, especially when you aren't sure how someone will react.

If you recognize that someone wants to speak with you more, it is also good to acknowledge this and create the right atmosphere where you can have a more in-depth discussion. Find a moment when you can fully concentrate on what they want to say, whether that is during a meeting or privately in your office.

How to Use Your Body Language and Micro Expressions to Be Congruent with Courage

To be taken seriously when you decide to speak up, think of yourself as speaking on a stage. To be noticed, you need to create a physical and emotional presence so that others will pay attention to you. Before you begin to speak, wait five seconds to create a bit of anticipation and to ensure the other person is giving you their full attention. Once you begin to speak, use a voice that is both confident and calm.

To get your message across clearly and accurately, it's important to take on a strong, comfortable position. Imagine standing in such a way that if someone were to try to push you over, you would not move. This involves engaging your core and legs to plant yourself firmly in place. This will convey strength to the other person, but it will also help you feel more confident as you speak. You can also move into a power stance for a few moments, which involves putting your hands on your hips and opening your chest. This can boost your confidence, but be careful not to overuse it, as it can distract from the conversation at hand.

It's also important to make sure your arms are relaxed, that you have a straight back, and that you are not slouching, as this can make you look fearful or unsure.

Review this table to learn more about which gestures and micro expressions support courage and which suggest a lack of courage:

BODY LANGUAGE AND MICRO EXPRESSIONS THAT INDICATE COURAGE	BODY LANGUAGE AND MICRO EXPRESSIONS THAT SUGGEST A LACK OF COURAGE
• Strong stance	• Slouching
• Relaxed shoulders	• Nervous smile
• Open hands	• Scratching or tapping with fingers
• Straight back	• Playing with hair
• Smiling with timing that indicates pride	• Smiling with timing that indicates contempt
• Surprise with timing that indicates delight or opportunity	• Surprise with timing that indicates fear or alarm
• Feet wide	• No eye contact

When looking at the table, keep in mind that there is a difference between confidence and arrogance. Confidence involves tapping into your own sense of strength, while arrogance is about using that strength to demonstrate superiority. If you use your body language to convey arrogance, you may receive aggression from others who do not want to feel inferior.

MICRO EXPRESSIONS OF SADNESS AND ANGER

When communicating courage it may be appropriate to use micro expressions to indicate anger or sadness if that supports the seriousness of the message. Of course, it's important not to go too far with this, as you don't want your listener to mirror any micro expressions of anger or sadness. Instead, you want to show just enough that helps them understand the importance of the situation.

●

How to Recognize Courage in Body Language and Micro Expressions Using the BLINK Technique

Here, you can use the BLINK technique to assess how ready people are for change, as change requires courage in many situations. Instead of asking this directly and risk receiving the answer that they believe you want to hear, you can analyze their response to various alternatives.

As an example, we can use the BLINK technique to assess how open a team member is to moving from the US to Germany to work as a representative for the company for a year. For the first alternative, you could say something like: "For some people in our company, it might be difficult to move to Germany with their family after they have built a life in the US. Working in a new language and integrating into a new culture can be a challenge, and it's not something that everyone would like to do. In this case, it would really help the company, but their personal life is more important to them, so they would prefer to change their job and receive a lower salary rather than move to Europe."

For the second scenario, you could say: "Other people at our company would be more adventurous and would like to move to Germany. As it's only for one year, they think it would be a great opportunity to have new experiences and make new friends. They understand that this move would help the company grow, and since they can be the one representing the company, it could be a great career boost, so they are happy to do it."

Pay attention to their response to each scenario. Do they frown or seem to shrink back when you talk about a big move from the US to Germany? Do they smile, open up, and appear excited about the possibility? Reading their reactions can be a good way to determine their level of courage in the face of change.

Integrating Courage into Who You Are

Integrating courage into who you are is a question of what you believe to be a meaningful life. You can choose to simply lay down and do what others tell you to do, following all of the preset rules and staying within the game that others have already started. Or you can be bold, creating a new game with new rules for yourself.

In my case, when I was in my twenties, I had a decision to make. I could follow in the steps of my parents or I could do something bolder and create something from scratch. I decided on the latter and started my own business. It required courage, but it also demanded that I work to overcome the limiting beliefs that I had absorbed through my family and friends. You may find that you take on limiting beliefs from those around you who want to keep you down because they are not courageous enough themselves to make bold changes in their lives. If you do that, it will be difficult to be courageous and take the big steps you need to take to do something new.

FINDING INSPIRATION

If your family and friends are limiting you more than supporting you, where can you find inspiration? When you are creating your own vision of who you want to be and the life you want to live, you can look at books, YouTube channels, social media pages, political leaders, business leaders, and so on. The important thing isn't necessarily where you find inspiration but that you find inspiration in those who are living the kind of life you want to aim for. If they can offer you a good example of things you should do to achieve your goals, use them as a source of inspiration.

For me, it worried me when I considered that I could be making more money than my father. This was less of a rational thought and more of an emotional one. In my culture, it's not easy to be better than your parents. My father had always wanted to be my mentor, and I ended up ignoring a lot of the wisdom he tried to share with me when I began doing things my own way. I was being bold, courageous, and different, but that left me quite isolated from friends and family. I had to find inspiration from people who had already achieved things I wanted to achieve and who had gone further than I had.

When I was first starting out, I found inspiration in a book by Joe Vitale. I used his methods as I was building my business, and it helped a great deal, as I could see the specific steps I needed to take. More recently, I have found inspiration in Marshall Goldsmith as someone who practices courage. When Marshall introduces himself during presentations or interviews, he always starts by saying that he's the number one leadership coach in the world. He's courageous about presenting himself in an authentic, bold way. He embraces who he is and who he wants to be, which is something I also strive to do.

WHICH ACTS ARE COURAGEOUS?

Acts of courage look different for everyone, but at its core, courage is about transforming something in your life. If you dream about changing your career to become a motivational speaker, a courageous act could be taking a course to get started. If your goal is to travel to a foreign country, a courageous act could be stepping onto the plane. Bold goals will always require courageous actions. It can be easy to spend a lot of time hesitating, overthinking, and ruminating on the steps you want to take. Courage is about moving past that and taking action. Once you move past thinking into doing, you will find that your mindset and energy changes, propelling you toward more courageous actions.

Also, don't forget that expressing yourself and sharing your opinions always takes courage. Whatever and whomever you believe yourself to be, say it, share it, and embrace it. That is the best way to integrate courage into your life.

●

Helping Others Integrate Courage into Their Lives

START EARLY

When it comes to helping others live their lives with courage, it's best to start early. If you have children, their early years can be a perfect time to start encouraging courageous actions, as they already have a natural ability and desire to speak up and share what they think and feel. Many children may start by crying or whining when they want something, and instead of shutting them down completely, you can use those moments to help them learn how to express what they want and why, which can be a crucial skill throughout their lives.

For example, my seven-year-old son has a dream of owning an electric guitar. At first, he started by nagging us and crying about the fact that he wanted a guitar. I had to explain to him that the way he was presenting himself wasn't the best way and that if he really wanted the guitar, he needed to use a calm voice, be kind, and present his passion and reasoning for wanting a guitar. After hearing this, he created a book about guitars, drew pictures of guitars, found names and styles of guitars that he likes, and calmly presented us with all this information during one of our meals. It was an open space where we were able to listen to him carefully and consider buying him a guitar.

COURAGE AND OPEN COMMUNICATION

It's easy to inhibit others from being courageous if you close opportunities for communication. For example, ignoring what others say or failing to take their ideas or the information they present into account discourages them from sharing more in the future. On the other hand, if you create an environment where they are allowed to share their thoughts and concerns, as well as what is important to them, you can encourage future moments of courage.

This idea is similar to what happens in therapeutic groups, as the information shared there is often more difficult for people to say. That is why those groups often create a circle where everyone feels equal and is presented with a safe space to speak. You can also practice this with your team members. During a meeting, for example, you can ask everyone around the table to share their thoughts on the current project, concerns they have about upcoming changes, and so on. If they feel they are in a space that is open and free of judgment and interruptions, it will be easier for them to speak in a courageous way. It's even better if their ideas and opinions are taken into consideration for future plans or decisions.

Another way you can promote courage through the sharing of ideas is by setting up a brainstorming session. For example, you can write down various opinions related to a specific project or policy and then ask your team members to play devil's advocate. Invite them to share any and all possible concerns, difficulties the team may face, things that could go wrong, or things that could prove harmful or hurtful to those involved. Make space for even the most bizarre complaints, concerns, and so on. Then, step back and discuss everything that was brought up, evolving the project in a way that includes all of the new information. After this process, people will be more motivated to work on a project if they have been given space to be courageous and voice their ideas in a safe space.

Remember that everyone has the ability to be courageous, and courage doesn't need to be a threat to a company. Not all revolutions start from fights. Some start from great ideas. By making space for those ideas, you can improve your team and your company.

CHAPTER SIX

DISCIPLINE

• • • • • • • •

In the opening scene of *An Earned Life*, the viewer sees Marshall Goldsmith on the phone, answering questions such as, "How many steps did you take today?" and "Did you do your best to find meaning?" What you learn later in the film is that this same routine happens every single day. His assistant checks in with him based on a list that Marshall himself has created based on what he hopes to achieve on a daily basis. This is how he maintains discipline in all that he does.

A BAD REPUTATION

In Western cultures, many people hear discipline and immediately think back to their days at school. The term has earned a bad reputation for this reason. But I'm not talking about discipline as it relates to punishment. I'm talking about discipline as it relates to dedication. When you practice discipline as it relates to your goals, you can sustain certain behaviors, such as eating healthy food for dinner each day, exercising each morning after waking up, or reading ten pages of a book before going to sleep. Therefore, discipline can be a positive factor in any life, especially the lives of leaders.

SMALL STEPS EVERY DAY

In the previous chapter, I talked about the Japanese philosophy of *kaizen*. While you certainly need *kaizen* to practice courage, you also need it to practice discipline. With small steps taken every day, you can achieve any goal. For example, nearly twenty years ago, I began to practice meditation. I started with just a few minutes every day—small steps that ended up taking me further than I ever expected. After two decades of daily practice, I live a calmer life, and I have more insight about what my priorities are as well as what my emotions are trying to tell me. I didn't see many benefits in the first weeks of my meditation practice, but looking back now, I can see just how far those small steps have taken me.

For Marshall, he devotes at least thirty minutes a day to writing and creating new material. Thirty minutes a day may not seem like much, but through that simple discipline, he has written three *New York Times* bestsellers and is currently promoting his fourth book (which may very well be another bestseller).

I'm a big fan of the Polish journalist Ryszard Kapuściński. He died in 2007, but during his life he is reported to have written only half a page of material each day. It seems like a small number, but it added up to nearly two dozen books that focused on his travels but also dove into the art of observation. His work is fascinating, and it all arose from the discipline of writing a little bit each day.

For many people, you can see that a daily, creative practice unclogs blockages that prevent creativity from flowing, which helps them create amazing works, such as the books by Goldsmith and Kapuściński.

THE PATH TO MASTERY

In his book *Outliers: The Story of Success,* Malcolm Gladwell famously asserts that the number of hours needed to master anything is ten thousand. That sounds like a lot, and it is. If you dedicated one hour every single day to a given skill, it would take you just under twenty-seven years to master it, based on Gladwell's assertion. *Twenty-seven years.* But if we take a step back, twenty-seven years is probably about a third of your expected lifespan. And at that point, you would be a master of whatever it was you had decided to work on and could use that mastery to improve both your life and the lives of those around you.

The point here, though, isn't to set a goal to be a master of a given skill. The point is that taking steps every day toward a particular goal will eventually lead you to achieve it. In the book, Gladwell states, "Success is a function of persistence and doggedness and the willingness to work hard for twenty-two minutes to make sense of something that most people would give up on after thirty seconds." As you have likely noticed, when someone you know begins an exercise routine, they usually last only a few weeks before abandoning it. Gladwell's point is that if you can become the person who keeps going after those few weeks, you can achieve true success.

A LONG-TERM VISION

As a leader, much of what you do requires a long-term vision and planning with that vision in mind. You need discipline to make sure you complete all the elements that will bring your vision to life. This discipline can be in the way you monitor the tasks you need to do every day, or as Marshall Goldsmith points out, it can be about making sure you're doing things each day that help you be a better version of yourself.

Top athletes train for hours every day to get in the best shape possible. Leaders need to develop discipline around their own "training" each day to make themselves and their team as good as they possibly can be. Discipline is not about quick success but about long-term achievements and the legacy you leave behind.

How to Recognize Discipline in Yourself and Others

Discipline comes about when you decide to do something and actually follow through with it. For example, maybe you decide you want to run every day before work. Discipline would mean waking up, putting your shoes on, and going for a run each day, no matter what else may be going on in your life.

By taking a look at the activities you're able to commit to, you can see how well you do when it comes to discipline. Think of a goal you recently set for yourself. Maybe it's eating healthier, painting each day, or spending more time with your family on the weekends. It can be anything. How well did you commit yourself to that goal? Did you prepare a healthy dinner each night? Did you paint half an hour every other day until you finished a painting? Did you play with your kids each Saturday afternoon? If you find that you were able to stick to your goal, you likely have a high level of discipline. If you started strong but eventually gave up on the goal, that could be a sign that your level of discipline is low.

THE DAMAGE DONE BY LOW DISCIPLINE

I have a friend who, at one point, became very enthusiastic about going to the gym. She kept telling me that the following month she would have the money to buy a gym membership and exercise clothes. She was planning to go to the gym three times each week to get in shape. When the time came, she did buy the membership and the new clothes, but she found herself only going to the gym once a week. She told me she didn't like the atmosphere of the gym and thought she would prefer hiking twice a month instead. This was simply an excuse that she used to hide her lack of commitment and the fact that she didn't have the discipline to follow through with the things that were important to her.

Those who don't practice discipline are clipping their own wings. In my friend's case, she wanted to be fit, but she didn't take the time to develop the discipline that would have helped her achieve that. It meant that she was often frustrated and disappointed in herself, and that negative energy spread into other areas of her life. It made her feel that her life was a failure because she couldn't achieve things that she valued.

When this happens, you are telling yourself that you are not good enough to achieve what you want. This lack of self-worth can damage your mental health. Therefore, one of the most important things you can do when you decide to improve your level of discipline is to offer yourself self-love by deciding you are important and worth the time it takes to fulfill your goals each day. Even if it's just five minutes each day of drawing, playing the piano, or listening to an educational podcast, those five minutes will take you closer and closer to your goal.

For my part, I use about five minutes each day to jump on my trampoline. It's a short amount of time, but it gets my heart rate up, and after just a few months of doing this each day, I noticed changes in my body. During those five minutes, I am choosing my health over easier activities like scrolling through social media or watching Netflix. I am practicing self-love and improving myself as a leader and person.

| 1 | 2 | 3 | 4 | 5 | 6 | 7 | 8 | 9 | 10 |

← ———————————————————————————————————→

LOW DISCIPLINE　　　　　　　　　　　　**HIGH DISCIPLINE**

This is a scale you can use to measure the discipline of each member of your team and then discuss what may need to be improved.

How to Verbally Communicate Discipline

When it comes to discipline, you need to share with others that you are committed and that this commitment is genuine. In my work, I speak with many businesspeople who will say they are interested in a particular project or agreement and that they will follow up soon. Often, weeks go by before I hear back from them with excuses about why they haven't been in touch. This kind of inconsistent communication *does not* demonstrate discipline. Once I realize they aren't actually committed to what they have spoken about, I decide it often isn't in my best interest to work with them long term, as this kind of inconsistency spills into other areas of work.

Therefore, to communicate discipline, the key is to follow up with what you say you will do. If you tell someone you will contact them before the end of the week, make sure that email goes out before Friday. If you tell them you will put them in touch with your business contact, take five minutes that afternoon to forward them that information. Empty promises kill discipline, so if you say you will do something, make sure you do it.

TRANSPARENCY AND DISCIPLINE

What happens if you aren't sure if you'll be able to follow through? You need to be transparent about that. Maybe you really like a proposal that someone brings you, but you aren't sure if you will have time to see it through. Tell them that. Communicate your interest while also letting them know that you aren't sure if time will allow you to commit. Plan to touch base within a few weeks to see how things have developed. It's always best to be upfront about what's going on in order to manage expectations.

DECIDE WHAT'S IMPORTANT

When you're communicating discipline to others, it's key that you have your priorities clear. What are you willing to practice discipline with, and what are you willing to let go of? If a project or task doesn't align with your priorities, it's important to communicate that, because if you commit to working with someone over a period of time, it will demand your time and energy. You need to know if it is worth it for you.

When you demonstrate what you are willing to devote time to, people will take you seriously when you say yes to a given project or task. They will trust your commitment and believe that you will be disciplined enough to carry your plans through. As a leader, it's important that your team members feel they can trust you when you tell them you will commit.

ENTHUSIASM AND DISCIPLINE AREN'T THE SAME

It's easy to mistake an enthusiastic attitude for discipline. When we see others get excited about the prospect of joining in on a particular project, participating in a given activity, or taking on a new responsibility, we can easily believe that they will be committed to that thing. But enthusiasm and dedication are not mutually inclusive. One can easily exist without the other. Excitement can begin to wane when responsibility sets in and the person realizes the extent of the commitment involved.

If you notice that someone often gets enthusiastic when you present new ideas but then rarely follows up with you about it, they're likely lacking discipline. On the other hand, you may find that there are people who are more reserved yet significantly more reliable, who will carefully consider what you place in front of them and communicate honestly about whether they want to commit. Those people will be easier to collaborate and work with on a long-term basis.

How to Use Your Body Language and Micro Expressions to Be Congruent with Discipline

The quality of discipline is about confidence. If you want others to take you seriously and trust that you will do what you say you will, you need to demonstrate confidence, honesty, and preparedness. These things all involve open body language, as well as directly facing the person you're speaking to. Placing your hands on your hips is a sign that you are ready, so this is a good thing to do when you want to show that you are prepared to take on what you have committed to. In Western or Arabic cultures, a handshake is also a positive gesture at the end of any conversation, as it acts as a kind of promise to deliver on what has been agreed.

On the other hand, displaying signs of fear, disgust, or contempt will suggest a lack of discipline and possibly convey that you have something to hide or want to cheat the person you are speaking to. Any body language that demonstrates uncertainty is also detrimental to discipline. For example, scratching your head is a classic sign of uncertainty. It is said that if you scratch your head with the right hand, it suggests a lack of the skills needed to complete what you have said you would; if you scratch your head with the left hand, it indicates a lack of belief in yourself. If you are feeling uncertain about what you are committing to, it's always better to discuss that before jumping in.

Review this table to learn more about which gestures and micro expressions convey discipline and which suggest a lack of discipline:

BODY LANGUAGE AND MICRO EXPRESSIONS THAT INDICATE DISCIPLINE	BODY LANGUAGE AND MICRO EXPRESSIONS THAT SUGGEST A LACK OF DISCIPLINE
• Eye contact	• Scratching head
• Nodding	• One eyebrow raised
• Easy smile	• Pressed lips
• Leaning forward	• Hiding behind an object
• Hands placed on hips	• Organizing objects while speaking
• Lips pressed in concentration	• Nose wrinkled in disgust
• Contempt that indicates pride and conviction	• Eyes wide with fear
• Sitting comfortably in chair	• Sitting on edge of chair

CREATING CONFIDENCE

What if you're feeling mentally unprepared for the task presented to you and aren't ready to commit? You need to create confidence by developing a plan and being realistic about the time and energy the task will require. Instead of being too optimistic, be more realistic and aware of any difficulties you may encounter. By doing that, you can plan for eventualities and feel more confident as they come up.

Once you have grown your confidence, you will be able to convey a greater sense of calm and be more cohesive with your body language, which will help others trust you and your abilities.

How to Identify Discipline in Body Language and Micro Expressions Using the BLINK Technique

It's crucial to know how disciplined other people are in order to choose the right people for a given project. When you choose them, you want to know they will be committed and deliver what they promise.

Many times, when people are trying to get a job or earn the responsibility of a new task, they will do just about anything, including exaggerating their skills and abilities. That's where the BLINK technique can be useful. By presenting different options and scenarios, you can directly observe how the person reacts and discern whether they really are ready to take on what you are offering.

PRESENTING VARIOUS SCENARIOS

There are two effective ways to use the BLINK conversation technique in this case. The first is, as I've shown in previous chapters, to present different scenarios of how people may react in the face of a particular challenge. Here, that would likely involve describing the various tasks they will be engaged with to see their response.

For example, you could start with an option like this: "Some of you might be very enthusiastic when the project begins, but as difficulties arise, you may feel overwhelmed. For example, some find it challenging to acquire new customers because there isn't much creativity involved, and receiving constant rejections can be mentally difficult. Cold calling requires a lot of discipline, as well as keeping detailed files about whom you have contacted and what response you have received. If you struggle with rejection, you may slow down the project. Forging new client relationships may sound easy, but it can get tiring very quickly, and if you get tired, you will slow down the overall project."

The scenario you present is more focused on the negative. Now you need to present a more positive scenario: "At the same time, with my experience working on this type of project, I know there are some people who love working on this kind of acquisition of new clients. They remember everyone's name and become fast friends with those they talk to. They become committed to making enormous numbers of calls, even if that involves working late some days. Rejections are unavoidable, but there are some people who meet rejection calmly and with a smile. Those are the people who will be successful with this project."

When using the BLINK technique here, your goal is to be able to discern between honest reactions of enthusiasm and reactions of uncertainty or discouragement. In the example, you may see micro expressions of fear appear when you begin describing the process of cold-calling and dealing with rejections. That person likely won't be a good fit for the position. On the other hand, if you see that they continue to smile and lean forward, they will likely be more prepared for the challenge ahead.

DESCRIBING TASKS

Here, instead of laying out scenarios, you could also consider making a list of tasks a project will include to see how people react when they see or hear the list.

For example, you may tell them: "This project is complex, and you'll be expected to juggle several tasks. One task is creating promotional materials, which requires creativity and research in order to search for slogans, check our competition's materials, and make our campaign distinguishable. Another task is to engage in cold-calling. You may need to call five hundred people to acquire the best clients. In this case, you'll need to face many people who will reject your call as you try to build new client relationships. Finally, you'll need to create spreadsheets to analyze who has responded to your outreach efforts and create calculations for further marketing analysis."

While you describe the various elements of a project, you can observe their movements and facial expressions. Do they seem to wince when you mention creativity? Do they shift in their seat when you talk about developing spreadsheets? If there are any signs of discomfort or fear, you may need to consider whether this person is the best choice for the project.

Integrating Discipline into Who You Are

Like Marshall Goldsmith's list of questions that he is asked by his assistant each day, it's important for you to be clear on exactly what it is you want to achieve and why. Marshall is committed to walking ten thousand steps each day because he knows it is good for his health. He has made his health a priority and decided that it is important enough to devote time to each day.

Therefore, to begin integrating more discipline into who you are, it's good to make a list of things that are important to you. Then, make a list of tasks that are related to those important things or values you have. If one important value you listed is family, for example, create action steps that will get you closer to spending more time with your family. For Marshall, that means taking the time to call his son or daughter every day. For me, it means committing to sitting with my children each evening to talk about what they did that day.

Different values will bring different action steps. For example, if one of your values is beauty, you may create an action step that involves creating a daily skin care routine. If one of your values is spending time in nature, perhaps your action step is planning one hike every two weeks. If one of your values is being a good leader, you may commit to talking one-on-one with one of your employees each day, even if only for five minutes. The commitment doesn't have to manifest each day. It can happen three days each week, or even once a month in some cases, but it must be consistent in order to produce discipline.

In the end, having discipline depends on having a good action plan and carrying out all the steps that are necessary to achieve your goal. You will be surprised in a year or two when you notice that those steps have carried you to a better version of yourself.

Helping Others Integrate Discipline into Their Lives

As with many of the qualities I've spoken about, as a leader, it's important that you act as an example of discipline. When people around you see that you are committed and determined to do what you set out to do, they will also want to ensure they are up to the task and able to meet your level of discipline.

BEING A SOURCE OF INSPIRATION

In your daily life, you may commit to picking up a piece of fruit when you want a snack. Soon, you will likely notice that your partner or children also start to choose fruit more often. They will be inspired by your example, sometimes even unconsciously. In general, people respond better when given the chance to follow an example instead of when being criticized or judged. Give them a chance to learn and do better, and they usually will.

For example, I was working on a professional project with a friend some time ago, and I soon noticed that she lacked many organizational skills. She struggled to manage her time and to keep her space tidy. Instead of complaining about this and the distraction it was causing, I decided to first try acting as an example. I kept detailed schedules, organized our work area, and laid out the steps we would take when communicating with clients. After a couple of days spent together, I noticed a change in her. She began to adapt and slowly became more organized. After a while, she even thanked me because she had realized that my example helped inspire her to improve this quality in herself. In the end, my positive example was much more fruitful than judgmental comments would have been.

FEEDFORWARD

Marshall Goldsmith is a great example of someone acting in a disciplined way and inspiring others to improve. Marshall has even built a technique around this called "feedforward" (as opposed to feed*back*). The idea is that instead of commenting on someone's past behaviors, which they can't change, you give "feedforward" about what they can improve in the future, based on their specific goals. He uses this technique with CEOs, who have reported that the exercise helps them focus on the positive things that they can improve upon instead of what went wrong in the past. It's a very powerful way to share our insights about other people's behavior without taking on a judgmental or critical tone.

IT'S SHOWTIME

In *The Earned Life*, Marshall Goldsmith talks about the concept of "showtime." He pointed out that those who were working on stage in New York had to repeat the same performance night after night. It didn't matter if they had a headache or were particularly tired or going through a tough moment emotionally. When it was showtime, they had to be on stage.

Marshall translated this concept to apply to an overall sense of discipline. When you commit to something, you put excuses aside and do what you've said you will do. Showtime is about doing what you have committed yourself to, independently of whatever else may be happening in your life. That is where true discipline lives.

CHAPTER SEVEN

INTEGRITY

● ● ● ● ● ● ● ●

While discipline helps to build trust, integrity can help to set it, like cement between bricks. For leaders, it often happens that the people around you watch your every step, not necessarily because they are waiting for you to make a mistake but because they are looking for a role model.

You may have noticed the way that many people seem to take political scandals personally, as if the perceived moral failing of this well-known figure were a personal insult. This is because people look to leaders to be role models for all of society. Many of the scandals we see around politicians happen when the individual has been "discovered" deviating from whom they claimed to be. It may be related to religion, sexual orientation, lifestyle, or just about anything. In most cases, if the person had simply been up front about it from the beginning, it never would have caused an issue, but the misrepresentation develops into a perceived lack of integrity.

Remember, integrity is about trust, so if leaders hide parts of their personality because they think it won't be good for their image, it is likely to cause problems when it comes out later, as people will feel they can't trust them. It's much better to be authentic and open about who you are from the beginning. If those around you can accept you with your human flaws, there will be nothing standing in the way of them trusting you without reservation.

DISCIPLINE AND INTEGRITY

Integrity also comes into play when someone makes a promise or commits to doing something. I spoke a bit about this in the previous chapter. When you commit to something and actually carry it out, you are demonstrating discipline, which helps people trust you. This also helps people see you as having integrity. They feel that when you say you will do something, you will do it—that you are a person of your word.

How you behave also connects to both discipline and integrity. If you lead people to believe you are a certain way, discipline helps you commit to things that bring out your true personality. Integrity ensures authenticity when you reveal who you are. For this reason, people can get very angry when they see someone doing something that doesn't seem to align with whom they believe that person to be. For example, you've likely seen cases where a TV personality who is often seen as calm or "in control" loses their temper and, as a result, loses a great deal of respect from their audience. It's not that people automatically dislike those with a temper. It's more likely that they feel betrayed because they thought they knew who this person was and are seeing a side that they feel was hidden from them. When you consistently act in a way that people feel is authentic, they will believe you to have more integrity.

LOOSEN THE RULES

You may be thinking that it is very difficult to always adhere to the kind of personality people believe you to have. Even when you're entirely authentic, everyone has moments when they get angry, say things they regret, or let their emotions lead them to make decisions they would rather have avoided. That's why it's important to make sure the rules around your behavior aren't too strict.

Perhaps you are a person who is generally down to earth and easy to talk to, but you also know that you occasionally lose your temper. Unless you show people that in small bursts from the beginning, they will lose respect for you later. If people know that it's a possibility from the get-go, a moment of anger will likely be quickly forgotten or forgiven. This is what I mean about relaxing the rules around your behavior. Create space for mistakes or out-lying emotions by showing people from the beginning that you're capable of those things.

CREATING YOUR PSYCHOLOGICAL SPACE

Another thing that helps integrity is to make sure you have your own psychological space where you can come back to yourself every day and tune into your own energy. This can be through meditation, walking in nature, listening to your favorite music, or anything that brings about an inner calm and allows you to connect to your true self. Think of your psychological energy like that of a laptop. Every laptop needs to be plugged in occasionally to recharge. You have to do the same for your psychological energy. Your personal activity is the outlet that provides access to the energy you need to recharge. Fortunately, you don't have to charge for as long as a laptop would; just five to ten minutes a day can help.

You can also find additional active ways to recharge. Doing sports can be a great way to move your body and connect with others. Getting together with friends and family is also ideal, as those are moments when you can be completely yourself and receive unconditional love. Try to seek out those kinds of moments at least once a week.

Every day at 10:00 a.m., I drink a small pot of high-quality Japanese green tea. It's a moment when I can tune into myself and my energy, but it's also a moment when I know I will receive unconditional love, as my cats never fail to join me for that special moment. I use this time to tap into insights, tune into my psychological energy, and recharge for those moments that can test my resolve. This helps me be the most authentic version of myself and maintain my integrity.

FEEL THE VIBRATION

As a leader, you likely work with many different kinds of people. It's important to make sure you can come back to yourself, because the people around you can come with very different emotions and energies from you. If they are angry, frustrated, anxious, or sad, those emotions and their associated vibrations can interact negatively with your own.

It has been shown through studies on radio waves and vibrational frequency that different emotions have different vibrations. For example, negative emotions have a more chaotic field of vibration. Think of yourself as an antenna for different vibrations. You can see the truth in this when you listen to a certain kind of music. If it's rock music, you'll likely feel more energized. If it's classical music, you'll likely feel more relaxed. That's all related to the vibrations of the musical notes interacting with your own energetic vibrations.

If you've had the experience of going to a sacred place, such as an ancient temple, you may also be able to relate to this idea. Upon walking in, how did you feel? Did you feel quieter or more attuned to your own thoughts? The people who visit these places are often those with a specific kind of energy built through personal reflection, prayer, or meditation. If you feel calmer upon entering that place, it's not just your imagination. The vibration of the place is working to induce feelings of calm within you. This can also happen with people. Have you ever met someone who seems to have a calming effect on everyone around them?

What kind of energetic effect do you want to have on those around you? Whatever it is, it should align with your authentic self. In a corporate environment, the energies tend to be quite heavy and disruptive, but they don't have to be. That's where the moments you take to recharge come into play, allowing you to remain within your own integrity.

How to Recognize Integrity in Yourself and Others

Your level of integrity is intertwined with how easily influenced you are by other people and how much change we can observe in our behavior over time. If you find that you generally act consistently, deliver on promises, and base your opinions on what you truly believe instead of what others tell you to think, you likely have a high level of integrity.

On the other hand, if you notice that you often shift your opinions without a good reason, struggle to make decisions, or are easily influenced by your environment and mood, you may have a low level of integrity. Those who struggle with integrity often don't think much about their values and instead choose to follow others in order to gain praise or other benefits.

To be a leader, you need to be able to stick to your values and keep your promises, and that requires integrity. Those who follow you want to know that you are predictable and dependable, that you will do what you say you will do. When they feel that's the case, they will respect and trust you.

USING VALUES TO GUIDE YOUR ACTIONS

As I mentioned before, integrity is about values. For example, imagine you get a job offer that comes with a more advanced job title and a raise, but would require you to work farther from home. If you value your family, you might not take that job because it would limit your time with them. If you value your career, you might take the job because it's a great opportunity with a higher salary. Integrity doesn't dictate which decisions you should make in every case; it simply acts as a guide when you have to make decisions that are related to certain values. If we aren't clear about our values, we may make decisions that create complications in our lives or even engage in self-sabotage. Integrity helps us prevent this by creating a guidebook for our behavior.

One of my great sources of inspiration for creating values in my life is John Demartini. His system of coaching and healing people on a profound emotional level is based on values. According to him, if you're aware of your top three values in life, then you are also able to solve most inner conflicts.

For example, between the time my son was born and when he turned three, I made three different movies. I was working a lot and giving most of my energy to my career because that's what my main value in life was. I hired three nannies and a cook in order to help me manage everything at home and give me time to focus on my work. But an interesting shift took place around the time my children turned four and two. At that time, my values shifted, and my main value became my family. I got rid of the nannies and the cook and instead hired a salesperson and an assistant for my business. I shifted my energy from my work to my family in order to spend more quality time with my children. I engage less with my business activities and am not as active in seeking out new opportunities as before, which allows me the time and space to participate more with my family.

The idea is not that some values are right or wrong. You simply need to decide what your values are so that you can build your life in a way that respects those and creates consistent, predictable behaviors built on integrity. If your values change, your actions can also change, but you need to know why so that you don't create frustration or guilt around the things you can't or don't want to do.

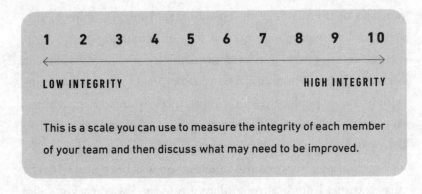

This is a scale you can use to measure the integrity of each member of your team and then discuss what may need to be improved.

How to Verbally Communicate Integrity

When thinking about how to verbally communicate integrity, it's crucial to be congruent with your words. Some years ago, I had a friend who changed her opinions and behaviors to fit a given situation. For example, with her friends she expressed views that were more politically liberal, while with her husband she was more conservative. When she got together with friends, she was a vegetarian, but at home with her husband she ate meat. At work, she was a reserved people pleaser, while at home she was the more dominant personality. She would essentially create distinct personalities for various situations and communicate very different ideas and opinions with different people. In doing this, she was undermining her own integrity, as it was difficult to know when she was speaking the truth as it applied to her.

On a verbal level, it's key to make sure you communicate similar information no matter the circumstance or person. Being the same person independently of where you are or who you are with requires courage, as it can make you vulnerable in certain situations; but it will help you maintain your integrity. Be clear about who you are and what you are willing to do, and it's likely that you will be accepted and respected without judgment.

SHIFTING YOUR IDENTITY

What happens if something in your life or personality must necessarily shift? How do you live this without lowering your integrity?

When I was twenty-two, I went on a seven-day *vipassana* meditation retreat. I felt transformed when I came back. I wanted to clear my mind and live a life with fewer toxins, which included alcohol. Being twenty-two, I had a group of friends, and we loved to party and drink together. I knew it would be a confusing shift for my friends if I didn't explain it to them, so I was open about what I had experienced. I explained the retreat and my new life goals. They understood that drinking alcohol was no longer aligned with who I wanted to be at that time. Because I was transparent, they were accepting and supportive of the change. I still spent time with them when they got together, even if I left earlier than most of my other friends, and it was never a problem.

This example demonstrates that if you explain your attitude, opinions, or lifestyle in a clear, consistent way, people will understand you and see you as a person of integrity.

AN INTEGRITY GAP

If you have children or have been around children, you may have noticed that if they don't get the answer they want from one parent, they will often go to the other in the hopes that they receive a different answer. Integrity can also exist in relationships, and children will often try to find gaps in integrity that they can take advantage of. In my home, my husband and I have a practice. When our children ask us something, only one of us is responsible for making the decision. For example, if they want to go to the beach one weekend, the parent who would be driving them would be responsible for making the decision, and the other parent would simply confirm what they have decided. In this way, we avoid giving contradictory answers and undermining the integrity we've built within our relationship and the relationship we have with our children.

The same can happen at companies. If there is no clear delegation of responsibilities, it can happen that there are miscommunications or misunderstandings based on different people giving different answers or information. To avoid this and create integrity in a company, there should be a clear sense of responsibility around who is in charge of which domains. If there is an instance where multiple people have to come to an agreement to make a decision, it would be important to delegate a spokesperson to avoid any contradictory answers.

STICK TO THE FIRST ANSWER

We can see another good example of integrity by looking at a typical habit of children. Have you ever noticed that a child will ask for something and, receiving a less-than-ideal answer, come back several hours later to ask again to see if the answer has changed? It often happens that a parent or caregiver will forget what answer they offered earlier that day and change what they tell the child. When a child knows this can happen, they will try to take advantage of it more often, as they see cracks in your integrity. In my family, we have taught our children that if we say no to something, that means no for the whole day. The answer won't change an hour or five hours later, no matter how many times they ask. This saves time and energy, and it also helps your children trust what you say.

The same is true in any business situation. If you tell a client or coworker something, you should remember what you said and stick to it. During calls or negotiations, take good notes and write down main points to avoid contradicting yourself later. If you change your response or position in the middle of a business interaction, it will suggest a lack of integrity. If you do decide that you must change something, it will require additional discussion to ensure that everything is clear and to keep your integrity intact.

●

How to Use Your Body Language and Micro Expressions to Be Congruent with Integrity

Integrity requires congruency between what we say and what we do.

Remember the body language congruency model? Detecting a mismatch between someone's body language and the words they use can be a sign of dishonesty. Others can also detect—consciously or unconsciously—when you are incongruent.

The body language congruence model is about creating congruence between what you say and what your body language suggests. For example, imagine meeting someone and saying, "I'm happy to meet you." In that case, body language congruence would suggest that your body language should be open and that your micro expressions demonstrate happiness. If you are showing micro expressions of disgust when you say that you are happy to meet someone, this shows a lack of congruence between what you are saying and what you are actually feeling. If one of your coworkers says, "I welcome all collaborations," during a meeting, but they have their arms crossed, this does not demonstrate congruence, as "welcoming" would involve open body language. In that case, there would be something they are feeling unsure about or uncomfortable with that requires more discussion.

A classic example of incongruent body language is Richard Nixon's infamous "I'm not a crook" speech. In just two minutes, Nixon's body language directly contradicts his words over and over again. Nixon says "I have never profited" but he nods yes with his head. He repeats the denial, but nods again. Then he says, "I have earned every cent," but betrays himself by shaking his head. He says, "In all my years of public life I have never obstructed justice," he first nods his head then shakes it. On the lines "Whether or not their president's a crook" and "I'm not a crook" he nods both times. When he again repeats "I've earned everything I've got," he shakes his head. On "I welcome this kind of examination," he shows his hands openly just briefly but quickly puts them away, attempting to show openness but not pulling it off, which is yet another sign of a lack of congruence. Over and over again, his words say the opposite of his actions. This is incongruence in a nutshell.

THE VISIBILITY OF INTEGRITY

For leaders such as politicians, TV presenters, and even CEOs, body language congruence is especially important, as a lack of congruence will be immediately visible and perceived as a lack of integrity. When you say something and don't believe it, it is very difficult to hide what you're feeling. We can think back to the example of Bill Clinton. Even though his micro expressions didn't give him away, the fact that he was incredibly tense and uncomfortable did. Suppressing emotions requires great effort and can be felt by those you're speaking to.

If you want to be congruent with who you are and build integrity, it's much better to be authentic and embrace your weaknesses from the beginning. Incorporate those things into the person you show the world, and it will be much easier to be congruent with your words and body language.

When it comes to body language associated with integrity, we must look at how open and comfortable someone seems. When someone is being congruent with what they say and do, they should look at ease. Review this table to learn more about which gestures and micro expressions suggest a sense of integrity and which suggest a lack of it:

BODY LANGUAGE AND MICRO EXPRESSIONS THAT INDICATE INTEGRITY	BODY LANGUAGE AND MICRO EXPRESSIONS THAT SUGGEST A LACK OF INTEGRITY
• Eye contact	• Looking away
• Open palms	• Hiding behind objects
• Relaxed posture	• Covering face by scratching or touching
• Belly area exposed	• Belly area protected
• Chest forward	• Body turned away, perhaps toward an exit

BODY LANGUAGE AND MICRO EXPRESSIONS THAT INDICATE INTEGRITY (CONT.)	BODY LANGUAGE AND MICRO EXPRESSIONS THAT SUGGEST A LACK OF INTEGRITY (CONT.)
• Sitting comfortably in chair • Smiling with both lip corners up	• Shifting from one side to the other • Smiling with only one lip corner up in contempt toward the other person

How to Recognize Integrity in Body Language and Micro Expressions Using the BLINK Technique

Imagine a team member has been given an assignment that they consider an undue burden. It is possible to communicate this with integrity, provided there is not excessive use of the second-person pronoun to imply that blame for this is being placed upon your manager.

For example, you could call up your manager and lay out some scenarios, testing the waters to see what would most persuade them to deny the client's request, for example.

"Some members of the team have expressed resistance to the assignment. I've heard some different voices on this. Some don't want to focus so much effort on one client to the exclusion of our other customers. Some feel like the new product is not living up to expectations and may even have disadvantages. Others feel like they are not prepared to take the extra overtime without additional benefits."

Observe the responses using the BLINK technique, and you'll gather vital data that could help you make your case.

It's possible to create too many negative emotions if you try to be confrontational while using BLINK, but in this case I did it on purpose in order to draw out a truth that someone was clearly trying to hide. If you see someone doing the opposite of what they claim, it may be a good time to use BLINK to confront them. But if you aren't sure, you can be more indirect and make the scenarios less confrontational, especially if the information is related to sensitive topics like politics or religion.

The goal of BLINK is to get to a place where you understand someone more and to check on certain characteristics, namely integrity in this case. Be gentle in order not to isolate the person you're speaking to, even if the scenarios create some tension or confrontation. Also keep in mind that going through the three scenarios should only take about five minutes, and afterward, you can lighten the mood by saying something like "I was just checking" or "I don't mind" in order to escape being confrontational for an extended period.

Integrating Integrity into Who You Are

I would like to come back to Marshall Goldsmith here because he is a person who is full of integrity. He demonstrates this by being honest about what he knows and what he doesn't. For example, if I ask him about something related to diet and health, he will simply respond that he doesn't know a lot about that. He would tell me that he can share his opinion but that he hasn't done any research in that area and can't share a well-informed response. This kind of transparency is key when it comes to integrity because in order to be true to who you are, you have to be willing to admit what your limits are.

YOUR AREA OF EXPERTISE

Nowadays, I meet a lot of people who try to be experts on everything and who share many superficial opinions. They write blogs or post these ideas on social media, even when they haven't researched the topic. The problem here is not only a lack of integrity; these things can also cause harm, as people may choose to follow the advice someone gives on a blog post. If the information isn't accurate or well researched, it could lead someone down a harmful path. Offering information when you haven't done the due diligence of looking into it contradicts your integrity, especially if you pretend to know a lot about a certain area just to appear intelligent. Some people may do this when they are afraid of losing others' respect and feel that they must put on an act. But this kind of deception is often easily discovered and can leave the person in a difficult position.

Marshall Goldsmith is an example of someone who owns up to his limits by admitting that he's not an expert on everything, and he has not lost any respect because of this. He claims to be an expert on leadership, and he is. People respect him for that and understand what information he has to offer. In the case of any leader, it's good to think about what your own area of expertise is and what you can share with the world. Instead of trying to be right about everything, which can cause a great deal of pressure, simply stick to what you're passionate and knowledgeable about in order to create integrity around that.

LOOK INTO YOUR VALUES

If you want to have more integrity, you must stick to your values. To do this, you must first decide what your values are. Look deeply into how you want to live, what's important to you, and how you want to share your individual message with the world. This is where it can be helpful to open up some time for creativity when you can tune into your true self.

If you are just getting started with building your integrity, I suggest you start small and grow from a couple of your most important values. Choose just two or three that you are willing to commit to. Make sure they are aligned with who you are, and slowly stop doing activities that contradict your values or that keep you from doing what you are passionate about. Over time, you will see that this brings more strength to your position and helps those around you communicate more effectively with you.

Keep in mind that you may lose a couple of friends in this process, as they may discover that their values don't align with yours. Embrace this, because being around those with values that conflict with your own will put you into conflict with yourself. It's much better to stick to your main values and surround yourself with people who can adapt to this. In the end, you'll feel that you are living a more fulfilling life this way.

Helping Others Integrate Integrity into Their Lives

When it comes to helping others build their integrity, it's important to be open to differences in opinions, behavior, and values. When you are open, you allow people to live within their own sense of integrity without feeling pressure to act a certain way. If what you want from someone conflicts with who they are, it will be difficult for them to maintain their integrity. For that reason, it's good to learn more about the people around you, especially related to their main values, so that you can act in a way that respects them.

We can see this in the example of a married couple with children. It's possible that one half of the couple would have values centered more on family, while the other may have values centered more on their career. If one person in the marriage gets frustrated by the other's focus and goals in life, it can cause difficulties in the relationship. Here, it would be key for both people to discuss their values and come to an understanding about what the expectations around these values are. If they are accepting of each other's values, they can live more harmoniously and without guilt. In this way, they can feel they are each being true to who they are and cultivating their own integrity.

We can also see this within corporations, where it's imperative to let people be themselves while trying to understand their main values. For example, if someone at a company values innovation, their tasks can focus more on creating new materials, and they can be invited to meetings meant for brainstorming. That person would likely thrive in that environment and feel that they are able to be their true self without having to fit the mold of another position. On the other hand, maybe there is another person who places more value on preserving traditions, and there is absolutely a place for that at a company as well. They can be involved in creating materials and activities that highlight the values and traditions of the company, which will, in turn, help the company preserve its own integrity.

As a leader, if you take the time to understand people's values and look for ways to help them focus on the things that are important to them, you can create a more productive, accepting environment for everyone.

PART 3

GROWTH SKILLS

CHAPTER EIGHT

HUMILITY

● ● ● ● ● ● ● ● ●

I n *The Earned Life*, the film exploring Marshall Goldsmith's
legacy, Marshall is seen speaking to James Feliciano, the vice
president of AbbVie Japan. He tells him, "Our mission in life
is to make a positive difference, not to prove how smart we are or
how right we are." This underscores the importance of humility
in Marshall's life. He has built his career on the idea that he must
continually earn respect and value without getting to a point
where he says, "Gee, I made it," and simply coasts on the reputation he has built up to that point.

This idea of earning your legacy every day can be a good way
to think about how humility can keep you on the right path as a
leader. Marshall is a leadership coach working with top CEOs
around the world. He's a leader in his field, yet he has set a goal

to remain humble in order to be able to connect on a personal level with everyone he meets.

Humility is a skill that allows you to stay in your own energy without boasting about your achievements or believing yourself to be better than those around you. While there are moments when you should present yourself as an expert in a certain domain, such as when you're interviewing for a job, it's important to focus on what you actually are an expert on and what you can bring to the table *as part of a team.*

When we were filming *The Earned Life*, I found Marshall to be incredibly easy to work with because he knew what he was an expert in and was also willing to acknowledge that I was an expert in the filming process. He did not try to intervene and was open to simply following the suggestions and guidelines that the film crew and I set for him. He was happy to offer insight when it came to content or what he would speak about because, in those moments, we were highlighting *his* area of expertise. When working with other experts during filming, it is often difficult for me to lead the process, as they try to comment on the way the film is being made or influence the direction it is taking. This often happens because they have a lack of humility and do not recognize that they can't be experts in everything. In the end, this makes collaboration more difficult.

WORKING WITH YOUR EGO

Humility is also related to how you perceive yourself in the world. It's about the ego. Some people have an inflated ego and therefore need to constantly prove themselves in order to make others see how intelligent or successful they are. On one hand, it may be important to share your achievements at certain times, but if you overdo it, those around you will find it difficult to connect or work with you.

If you are trying to sustain a big ego, it takes a great deal of energy, which doesn't allow you the energy to work on your relationships, be curious about others, or support those around you in times of need. A big ego will push others out of your space, which will interfere with every relationship you try to create or maintain.

I began to recognize a problem with my own ego when I was skiing. Often, during the first hour or so of my time on the slopes, I would focus on showing everyone how good of a skier I was. I would try to demonstrate my skill and speed, and I actually found that this caused me to have more accidents because my focus wasn't where it should have been. By focusing on showing off the skills I had, I was limiting the skills that I could continue practicing in a productive way, and I wasn't getting better. I had to retrain myself to release my ego, focus on the flow that I could enter when skiing, and have fun. I find that I still experience a few minutes at the beginning where I want to show off my skills, but I've gotten better at entering a space where I can focus more on skiing as an activity, and this has led me to enjoy it more and actually get better over time.

When I learned how to be humbler when skiing, I was able to connect it to being humbler in other areas, such as in my career. I realized that when I don't feel the need to impress others and show off, I can use that energy to take action and build relationships, which helps me feel better and helps others respect me more. People prefer to interact with those who are humble because they are the ones who will respect others and give them space to develop their ideas. This can create a wonderful collaboration and more productive work.

How to Recognize Humility in Yourself and Others

Your level of humility can be measured by how much you worry about what others think of you. If you spend a lot of time trying to impress others, reliving past conversations in order to figure out what the other person may have been thinking, or considering ways you can demonstrate your expertise, you likely have a low level of humility. Those who lack humility spend a lot of time thinking about how to win over others, gain a better position, or present themselves in a better light. These are all indications of a big ego.

It can happen that people consider humility to be a negative trait because they think that humble people are shy or lack confidence. This is a misconception. Humble people are simply more comfortable being who they are without trying to force that on others, so they may not be as fast to offer their thoughts or opinions if they feel it isn't the time or place. Those who practice humility focus on what is aligned with their own values and say and do only things that are in line with their goals. They complete tasks to support their team and in order to be a positive asset to their company, not to demonstrate their intelligence or special abilities.

THE FOCUS OF THE HUMBLE

We can compare humble people to an artist. Imagine a painter who is deeply focused on working on what is right in front of them, in mastering their art, in experiencing the process of creating a wonderful painting. They don't care about the external world at that moment. They care only that they are doing something they enjoy and getting better at it. Humble people, like that artist, are passionate about what they do and do it in the best way possible. This is a great strength because then they don't allow outside influences or critiques to diminish their art. Humble people are artists of their own domain.

Leaders who practice humility can master processes that they are strong in. Humility allows them to commit to a project or activity and focus on completing it because they don't worry about the criticism or feedback they will receive later. Humble leaders are self-confident and give a lot of energy toward focusing on their own goals and activities. Because of this, they can say no when it's needed. At the same time, they have space to listen to others because they are not busy acting from inside their ego.

WHAT GOT YOU HERE WON'T GET YOU THERE

In Marshall Goldsmith's book *What Got You Here Won't Get You There*, he discusses quirks that can inhibit a leader's success.

Some of them are related to problems associated with a big ego, as leaders with this problem stop thinking about others and single-mindedly pursue greater achievements. The attitude of an achiever is different from that of a leader. An achiever wants to impress others, show off, and be seen as the best in a group of people. A leader doesn't need to do these things, as they are there to serve others. A leader recognizes that they are already on top and so don't need to continue trying to best others. Because leaders have already arrived at a place where they can serve others in a meaningful way, they can focus less on themselves and practice gratitude for their position.

THE ROLE OF GRATITUDE IN HUMILITY

Gratitude can help great leaders be humbler because it helps them see how they can be of service to others, and leadership is ultimately about service. A leader is there to manage an organization, be attentive, listen, and take the advice of the experts they have brought into their team. With gratitude, you can feel appreciative toward those who are willing to help you and guide them through your own knowledge.

Gratitude weakens the ego, which attracts more people. People will try to knock you down if they perceive you as having an ego that is too big. But if they see you as being humble, they will want to help you. This means that, paradoxically, humble people hold more power and will always come out on top.

| 1 | 2 | 3 | 4 | 5 | 6 | 7 | 8 | 9 | 10 |

← ———————————————————————————————— →

LOW HUMILITY   HIGH HUMILITY

This is a scale you can use to measure the humility of each member of your team and then discuss what may need to be improved.

How to Verbally Communicate Humility

In the previous section, I mentioned the important role of gratitude in humility. When communicating humility verbally, gratitude becomes a central element. If you can be grateful about your life, about what others do for you, and about the things that bring you happiness, you can embrace how much you have achieved. But it also helps you think about others and their role in your success. Gratitude can push you to thank others, which can demonstrate humility, as you are recognizing that your achievements are possible only with support from others.

HOW GRATITUDE OPENS UP MORE POSSIBILITIES

When you give others space to share their ideas instead of always forcing your ideas into a conversation, you expand possibilities around what can be achieved. When you then thank people for their contribution and for supporting you and/or the project, you demonstrate an ability to be humble, even in the face of great success.

Gratitude is empowering. If you can empower others by expressing your thanks, you can help the energy rise. This can be felt on special holidays like Thanksgiving, for example, when we feel closer to those around us and experience gratitude for all the positive things in our lives. When gratitude comes into play, you can feel the energy around you shift in a more positive, productive direction.

WHEN TO SHARE YOUR ACCOMPLISHMENTS

If you are someone with a big ego, you feel the need to share a lot about yourself and your achievements. When you practice humility, you learn to decide when it's important to share your achievements and when it's better to hold that information back.

Years ago, I finished my master's in law, and, of course, I got my friends together to celebrate with a big party. The following year, I finished a second master's, this one in psychology, and organized another big party to celebrate my achievement. A couple of years after that, I received a third master's, this one in anthropology. This time, I decided to forego a party, as I felt that it would be akin to boasting. I was proud of myself and had deeply enjoyed the three master's programs, but I had chosen to pursue them for my own learning and goals, not to show off to those around me. Even now, when I am in a situation where I need to share my qualifications for a particular job or project, I will choose one or two of my master's degrees to include, depending on the area of expertise needed.

It's important to think about why you have chosen to pursue a given achievement. Are you doing it for yourself or for others? If you are doing something because you find it enjoyable or are curious about that area, you are on the right track. If you are achieving something to show off or prove you can to others, it may be time to think harder about what you really want from the goals you're pursuing.

HOW CONVERSATION SPACE IS USED

I work with hundreds of experts and speakers for the movies I make, and it's easy to notice the difference between those who are humble and those who have a big ego. Those who lack humility take up much more space in any conversation. They fill the time talking about themselves and don't leave space for those around them to share their ideas or brainstorm for the project at hand. I often walk away from those conversations feeling exhausted or frustrated.

On the opposite side are those who practice humility. They are easy to identify, as they are open and curious about my opinions, which makes any collaboration much smoother. If a person is attentive to what you say and can connect their ideas to what you are expressing, they likely have a high level of humility, which will make it possible to work toward a common goal during a conversation. People who are humble will naturally have more productive conversations because they know how to express their ideas while also leaving space in the conversation for others to do the same. They insert their expertise when it's needed and remain quiet when it's not. Their strength comes from the respect they give to others, which earns them respect in turn.

●

How to Use Your Body Language and Micro Expressions to Be Congruent with Humility

Self-confidence is key in humility, so those who demonstrate signs of self-confidence will often be those who show signs of humility. When self-confidence is taken too far, however, it can turn into arrogance and a big ego.

Body language associated with a big ego is that which asserts a sense of dominance. This can be seen in micro expressions of contempt, using an overly forceful hand in presentations or during a handshake, or raising the chin. Another sign of dominance is putting a hand out with the palm facing down. The hand gesture made infamous by Adolf Hitler is the most striking example of this, as it was used (quite effectively) to assert dominance among the Nazis.

One prominent sign that someone is practicing humility is an inclined head. If you notice when you are talking to someone that they incline their head slightly, opening up their neck, this expresses vulnerability and openness. It shows that they are listening to what you are saying and considering your thoughts and opinions. If you pay close attention when watching videos of Barack Obama's presidential debates, you will notice that he inclines his head often to indicate that he is listening to his opponent. This also works to calm any anger or negative emotions that may have been building, as it is a sign of respect.

Review this table to learn more about which gestures and micro expressions suggest a sense of integrity and which suggest a lack of it:

BODY LANGUAGE AND MICRO EXPRESSIONS THAT INDICATE HUMILITY	BODY LANGUAGE AND MICRO EXPRESSIONS THAT SUGGEST A LACK OF HUMILITY
• Eye contact	• Looking down on other person
• Open palms	• Hands behind head or back
• Relaxed posture	• Chin raised
• Inclined neck, showing main artery	• Hand extended with palm facing down
• Leaning forward	• Using overly forceful hand to shake hands
• Happiness micro expression with both lip corners up	• Uneven smile with only one lip corner up (a micro expression of superiority)
• Sitting comfortably in chair	• Shifting from one side to the other

MAKING FRIENDS AND ENEMIES

Practicing humility is key in offering respect and encouraging those you speak with to be more open and transparent with you. For that reason, humility is a quick way to invite people into your circle and make friends. On the other hand, those who project a big ego can quickly earn enemies, especially among top leaders, as they will not take well to projections of superiority.

In companies nowadays, leaders often try to achieve a sense of equality among team members, so arrogance and superiority will cause discord in any group. Humility, on the other hand, can increase collaboration and create a more welcoming atmosphere.

How to Identify Humility in Body Language and Micro Expressions Using the BLINK Technique

When using the BLINK technique to check for humility, the most important thing would be to observe how much the other person wants to impress people and how much they engage in activities because it's something they genuinely want to do or find necessary.

For the first scenario, you can describe someone who lacks humility: "For some people, their external image is very important, and they would do anything to get a better position and impress others, even if that means sacrificing their own needs or other projects. They often spend too much money on things that they think will give them a better social status or position in their workplace. They speak constantly about their achievements because they believe that others will remember them and collaborate more with them if they know these details."

As a second scenario, you can talk about someone who is humbler: "Other people focus more on creating real relationships with people they like and won't try to please others just to get something they want. They tend to be experts in their field and will show this only when it's needed. They don't talk much about their own achievements because they know it will come up at the right time. Instead of spending money on things that will impress others, they buy things because they're useful and because it makes them happy. They are generally good listeners and will hear others out."

When talking about these two different kinds of people, observe how the listener reacts. Do they seem to relate more to the first scenario or the second? If they smirk when they hear about someone who doesn't boast about their achievements, they may struggle with humility, for example. Which scenario seems more interesting to your listener and which bores or frustrates them? By observing this, you can gauge their level of humility.

Integrating Humility into
Who You Are

When thinking about how to increase your level of humility, it's important to notice how much time you spend impressing others. When you buy a new painting for your home, for example, do you imagine what people will say about it when they walk in, or do you think more about the pleasure you will get from looking at it each day? The concept of minimalism has grown from the idea that we buy much of what we do to impress others; the idea is that when we get rid of the desire to impress, we don't need as many things. Whether we can do this is tied into whether we have a big ego, as those with a big ego put a lot of money, time, and effort toward their external image. Ironically, most people are too busy with their own lives and goals to care much about the image others are trying to project.

LEARNING TO SHARE

A lack of humility can get in the way of genuine connection. When you struggle with a big ego, you will tend to talk too much about yourself, which can be annoying and off-putting for others, as they won't be able to find the space to share their own thoughts. If people feel they aren't being heard, they will also feel you don't respect them, which will get in the way of any desire or ability to connect.

If you can create an atmosphere where sharing and respect are the top priorities, this can lead to much better relationships and friendships. If you know that these qualities are things you struggle with, next time you're with others, time yourself to see how long you talk, and be mindful of how much the other person talks to see if there's a good balance or not. When trying to create new relationships, it's important to listen at least as much as you talk. With this in mind, you can practice changing your talk-listen ratio and allow more space for the people you talk to, which can increase your level of humility.

GIVING UP CONTROL

With children, it's easy to notice that they often don't talk for too long. They tend to share quick messages and then move on to their next activity. If you want to work on giving children more space to share their thoughts, it's more about showing than sharing. It's easy to overtalk your child, so change in this area would involve talking and instructing less and giving them more space to simply explore and be themselves.

The same is true in companies. As a leader, it's important to give your employees and team members the space to work and explore their abilities without being constantly observed, instructed, or judged. When you lower your own ego, you can trust that others will do a good job without needing to micromanage them. When your team members feel that you trust them, they will be more confident and do a better job with the projects they're given. Your role in that case would be to release some control and focus on being grateful for the effort they put into their work. You can then observe if this increases motivation among your team. Often, when given more space, people will flourish, and it will not devolve into chaos.

When you practice humility and allow people to take responsibility for themselves and their work, this also eases your workload, as you simply need to be present, not overbearing. A big ego will push you to do too many things out of fear that others won't be able to do them as well, so when you release your ego, you can shift the energy in your company and make space for others to manage more of their own work.

●

Helping Others Integrate Humility into Their Lives

Listening and showing respect to others can help calm their desire to show off. This can be seen in environments that promote competition, as those environments tend to attract and create larger egos. In more casual, open atmospheres, people let go of this and feel more able to practice humility. Therefore, as a leader, if you create an atmosphere that feels more casual and accepting for your team members, you can offer them the space to further develop the skill of humility.

I saw this myself when I was studying in various departments for my master's degrees. For example, in the law department, it was common for people to wear formal clothes and own nice watches and cars in an attempt to demonstrate their achievements. In the department of psychology, the goal tended more toward uniqueness, where colorful clothing or hair was not uncommon. If you could show how unique you were compared to others, it would help your status. In the department of sociology, it felt the most natural because the focus tended to be more on demonstrating knowledge instead of showing off through your choice of clothing, jewelry, or possessions. There was more curiosity there, which promoted more humility.

CREATING AN ATMOSPHERE OF JOY

A large ego is often related to fear, frustration, anger, or anxiety. A person's ego grows when they are afraid to lose something, such as the respect of others. One way to counter this is to create an atmosphere that promotes understanding, mindfulness, and joy. When people can focus on what they like and center themselves on positive emotions, it can calm their egos. If you allow others to feel safe in their own skin, you can not only promote humility but increase collaboration, as there will be more understanding between opinions and an openness to what everyone has to offer.

HOW HUMILITY IS VALUED

During my visits to Japan, I have noticed a stark contrast to the way they approach their egos. In general, Japanese people don't want to draw attention to themselves through colorful clothing or a loud voice. They do their best to melt into the general atmosphere and tune into others. This is quite different from the US, where those who speak the loudest in a meeting or those who wear the most striking suit would be the one that everyone pays attention to. In that case, those with a bigger ego would likely take the lead.

In Japan, big egos are not appreciated and rarely rewarded. Humility is highly valued, and Japanese people practice this by making sure they don't take too much talking space and demonstrating gratitude as often as they can. Because of this, I always feel more at ease in meetings in Japan, as they offer me space to share my ideas; and in turn, this helps me to realize when I need to offer space to others. When this kind of collaboration happens, it allows each individual to connect more to their inner motives and to understand what will drive them in their work and life, which can help them distance themselves from their ego.

CHAPTER NINE

POSITIVITY

● ● ● ● ● ● ●

Positivity is about being able to see the world as a place of expansion. When we are afraid or experiencing stress or anxiety, we see the world as contracting, closing in on us. When we are relaxed, positive, joyful, we can see the world around us as being more open and welcoming, full of possibilities.

You can see this on the body language level, as well. When animals are afraid or stressed, they close up to protect themselves. On the other hand, when they are relaxed or happy, they open up and get bigger, as they don't need to hide.

Positivity is a mindset that affects your whole body and the way you look at and interact with the world. If you can practice positivity, you can be more open to what the world has to offer.

THE SEA TURTLE

There was a day some years ago when my husband and I went to the beach. On that particular day, I was very tired, as I was busy with several work projects, and I was stressed because I was worried about not getting paid for some recent training sessions I had managed. My energy was very negative. As I was lying on the beach that afternoon, my husband came running over to me and said he had seen a sea turtle pass so close to him that he had been able to touch it. He was happy and wanted me to join him to see the turtle, to experience the joy it had brought him. It took me several minutes to find the energy to get up from my place on the sand and make my way to the ocean, and by the time I got there, the sea turtle was gone.

The sea turtle became a symbol for me, a reminder that these kinds of moments happen only once. You don't see a sea turtle up close every day, much less touch one. Because I had allowed my negative energy to keep me stuck, I hadn't taken advantage of what could have been a very special moment.

A few days ago, I took my children to the beach. I was also tired on that day, as I had been working in the morning, and all I really wanted to do was rest on the sand. But when my son came running over to tell me he had found a huge crab on some nearby rocks, I didn't hesitate before jumping up to go see it with him. We went to see the crab, walked along the beach, listened to the waves as they hit the sand, and in the end, I felt revived. My tiredness dissipated, and I realized that by taking advantage of the opportunity to see the crab, I had created not only a positive moment with my children but a positive memory to carry forward as well. If I had stayed on the sand that day, it would have been another unremarkable day at the beach, but my impulse to take action turned it into a joyful day.

THE LIGHT OF THE LEADER

As a leader, you are the one holding the torch for everyone to follow, and it's important that the torch burns brightly. Positivity is what gives more brightness to the torch's light. If a leader can develop positive energy and believe in future success, the whole team will follow with the same attitude.

When a leader is absent minded, tired, or frustrated, the light of their torch dims. They won't be able to see the sea turtle, as they'll keep themselves stuck where they are, which will keep others stuck as well. If a leader is able to dig deep, even on the tough days, and find extra energy for positivity, they can brighten their own life and the lives of their team members.

Positivity, as a light, doesn't distinguish between beautiful and ugly places. It will shine on everything. This light can transform glum moments into something brighter and bring them to life, even when stress or anxiety is trying to do the opposite.

How to Recognize Positivity in Yourself and Others

Positivity is often easy to identify based on a person's energy level. Those who have a low level of energy and who are generally resistant to change or close minded can be considered to have a low level of positivity. If you know someone who is constantly complaining, avoiding certain tasks, or keeping themselves stuck in the status quo, you've likely experienced what it's like when someone rates low on the scale of positivity.

A lack of positivity usually isn't an innate trait but something that sprouts from frustration, stress, or fear. When we get stuck in low levels of positivity, it can be hard to go the extra mile, be proactive, or make new, surprising decisions.

On the other hand, those who rate high on the scale of positivity generally demonstrate high levels of energy. They tend to be very proactive, approach new tasks with enthusiasm and curiosity, and believe in making changes. Those who embody positivity can see that there's always a way to solve a problem, and they have the energy to search for the solution, brainstorm, and try alternative ideas. They are always moving forward through open, creative thinking, emitting an air of positivity everywhere they go.

SEEING POSITIVITY IN YOURSELF

If you want to know whether you rate low or high on the scale of positivity, look at a simple daily task you are faced with. When you are asked to do something that is outside of your routine, how do you react? Do you approach it with enthusiasm and interest, or are you reluctant to step outside of the box you've created for yourself?

If you work at a company or corporation, you've likely known those people who are the first to answer questions, take on extra tasks, and open spaces for creativity. Those are the people who rate high on the positivity scale. On the other hand, there are those who tend to hide behind their desk and do their work but rarely approach new tasks with interest. They wish to stay where they are in both the short and long term, which is a sign of low positivity.

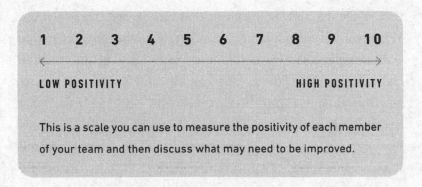

This is a scale you can use to measure the positivity of each member of your team and then discuss what may need to be improved.

How to Verbally Communicate Positivity

Being positive in business begins with focusing on a broader definition of success. Success comes about more naturally when you work to be intentionally positive, as those who do this seek achievement and feel they have a purpose. They believe in growth and prosperity.

Those who are positive intentionally avoid negative thoughts and self-criticism. Instead, they talk more about the possibilities and what needs to get done in order to be successful with a project or job. They discuss the mission and the purpose of what they're doing in order to create a broader vision for those around them.

THE THOUGHTS THAT MAKE THINGS GOOD OR BAD

Creating a vision is more difficult for those who focus on the negative, as they tend to have tunnel vision, homing in on what they're feeling and the problem that has caused those feelings. When you are in that kind of mindset, it can be easy to feel that everything is going wrong. Spilling your coffee, getting stuck in traffic, or arriving late to work can all cause you to think more negative thoughts and interact with the world in a way that makes things even worse. The same things may happen to someone who is more positive, but they will see them as passing inconveniences or even possibilities. Getting stuck in traffic, for example, could offer time to listen to an interesting podcast. It's about approaching both good and bad experiences with a mindset that allows you to see the world in a way that is positive and productive. Different reactions will create different results.

MAKING THE MOST OF IT

Those who are able to remain more positive tend to talk more about joyful moments. They may be considered more successful, but this is usually due to the fact that they make the most of each experience and take more initiative when they see an opportunity.

People who succumb to negativity often won't take initiative because they may not believe they'll be successful. They'll stay stuck where they are, which can cause others to get stuck as well. This kind of thinking can be contagious, which is why it's so important to look out for it at any company.

As a leader, you have the power to counterbalance negative energy with positivity by focusing on the mission and vision of your team. By describing goals and how to achieve them, you can show others a path they can follow, which will help them think more positively about what's at hand. One negative person can ruin a whole team, so a leader must represent a positive mindset that others can follow despite any difficulties they may be facing. The key is to focus on lessons that can be learned from mistakes or struggles, as well as solutions to problems that come up. Practicing positivity means focusing more on the possibilities and goals of the future and less on the mistakes of the past.

How to Use Your Body Language and Micro Expressions to Be Congruent with Positivity

Body language and micro expressions that convey positivity are centered on openness and enthusiasm. Those who rate high on the positivity scale will demonstrate a higher level of energy, and their faces will be covered in micro expressions of positive emotions, such as happiness or excitement.

On the other hand, those with a low level of positivity will demonstrate body language and micro expressions centered on avoidance, resignation, or resistance. This will cause them to close up, demonstrate superiority, or attempt to leave a situation that causes them discomfort.

Take a look at this table to learn more about specific gestures and micro expressions that demonstrate positivity and which demonstrate a lack of it:

BODY LANGUAGE AND MICRO EXPRESSIONS THAT INDICATE POSITIVITY	BODY LANGUAGE AND MICRO EXPRESSIONS THAT SUGGEST A LACK OF POSITIVITY
• Eye contact	• Crossed hands or arms
• Smiling with muscle around the eyes contracted	• Pointing with finger
• Nodding	• Palms down or "pushing" away from body
• Relaxed posture	• Touching nose/scratching head
• Leaning forward	• One eyebrow up (disbelief)
• Hands on hips (preparedness)	• Weak handshake (resistance)
• Hand gestures (enthusiasm)	• Facing door or packing up documents (avoidance)
• Facing the other speaker (engagement)	• Uneven smile with only one lip corner up (a micro expression of contempt)

BODY LANGUAGE AND MICRO EXPRESSIONS THAT INDICATE POSITIVITY (CONT.)	BODY LANGUAGE AND MICRO EXPRESSIONS THAT SUGGEST A LACK OF POSITIVITY (CONT.)
• Happiness micro expression with both lip corners up	• Disgust shown with a wrinkled nose
• Open hands showing inside palms	• A neutral expression— "poker face"

How to Recognize Positivity in Body Language and Micro Expressions Using the BLINK Technique

To use the BLINK technique to observe positivity, you can focus on presenting one idea instead of several options. The key is to include many details about the task or project, as well as outline the procedures involved. In this way, you can observe how your team members react to various elements of the described project.

As an example, assume the new project aims to increase sales by 30 percent in the next quarter. First, you need to present the idea: "Our goal is to increase sales by 30 percent in the next quarter of the year. The first task is to increase customer engagement, which means you'll need to double the number of follow-up calls you make each week. We will also need to send out more questionnaires, and you will need to ensure they are received via email and that as many people as possible fill them out, as this offers important insight about what our customers need. You will also need to select customers to call in order to get more information on their opinions. All of this will necessitate creating spreadsheets and calculating statistics from the questionnaires. After we have the results of the calculations, we will come together to brainstorm how to bring in more product variations for our clients, which will lead to another round of questionnaires and calls. Within three months, we hope that these steps will increase sales by 30 percent."

Notice that many specific details are given about what will be expected during the course of the project. While sharing each element, you can observe your team members to see how they react. How do they react when you talk about doubling the number of calls? Sending out questionnaires? Creating spreadsheets and completing calculations? Pay close attention to the level of enthusiasm and resistance around each element. The elements that seem to cause more resistance will need special attention in order to increase the level of positivity around them. When you see which people are the most enthusiastic, you can offer them an extra role or task where they will be likely to spread enthusiasm and encourage participation.

When observing resistance around certain parts of the project, it's important to take it a step further to find out *why* there is resistance. For example, if you know that your team members are resistant to increasing the number of phone calls they make each week because of a lack of time, you can brainstorm solutions to this. When everyone feels that there are measures in place to make the project go as smoothly as possible, their level of positivity will increase.

●

Integrating Positivity into Who You Are

When you want to increase your level of positivity, it's good to take notice of any negative thoughts and limiting beliefs you have on a daily basis. Scientists have estimated that we have around sixty thousand thoughts a day. Most of these thoughts go unnoticed, as they are produced out of habit. Therefore, when we take the time to slow down and notice them, we regain the power to change them into more positive thoughts.

A good way to do this is to keep a journal. Set an alarm clock to go off five or six times each day, and at those times, write down whatever it is you're thinking. After a week or two, you will have a list of thoughts that will allow you to see whether they skew positive or negative. If you identify any common negative thoughts or limiting beliefs, you can prepare to change them.

TRANSFORMING NEGATIVE THOUGHTS

One limiting belief that I struggled with for many years was the idea that achievement could come only through hard work and struggle. This led to me working harder than I often needed to for the same result, as well as feeling guilty when I wasn't working as hard as I could at something. For example, when I was studying, if I got a good grade after studying for only an hour, I would feel like a fraud, especially if I had friends who studied all week and got a lower grade. I was focused on how difficult it should be to succeed without thinking about the quality of the work I was producing. Over time, I was able to shift this thinking, realizing that there were times when I was simply studying more efficiently or working on a topic that came more naturally to me, which meant that I wouldn't need to work as hard. And this was okay.

If I had stayed stuck in this limiting belief, I would continue to feel guilty with each achievement. I would also seek out areas where I could take on extra work, despite already being quite busy. Fortunately, I realized how this thought was affecting my life and I stopped feeling like a fraud when I achieved something with less effort. This led me to compare myself to others less often, which was a relief because I could finally unlock my full potential by discovering the optimal pace for my life. I understand now that I don't need to struggle all the time; I can achieve the same things with a sense of ease and joy. This simple truth allowed my life to completely evolve.

When you identify a limiting belief or negative thought, decide on a positive thought or belief that can replace it, but don't stop there. You need to work on it consistently. Write down the new thought and keep the paper somewhere visible. Pay attention to it several times a day and consciously shift your mindset to accommodate it. You'll notice that when you are able to change your negative thoughts over time, positivity comes more easily.

Helping Others Integrate Positivity
into Their Lives

It's important to remember that most people who engage in excessive negative thinking often aren't aware of it. Years ago, I was working with a new coworker, and she would start her day with a neutral energy. Within a couple of hours, however, she would begin to criticize and complain about various parts of the project or the people working on it. I observed this for several days and quickly got fed up with it, as it was making the work more and more difficult to complete. I decided I had to confront her about her lack of positivity. I told her that working with her was impossible, as I couldn't stand the constant negative thoughts and criticism. I asked why she didn't believe in the project or want to do the work in the best way possible.

This confrontation ended up being crucial because she hadn't realized that she was being so negative. She told me that she had previously worked in a tense environment, which had cultivated negative thinking, and she thought this was normal. She came back several hours later and apologized and expressed a desire to change. She began observing the way I approached the project we were working on, and we were soon able to work together without issue.

Keeping in mind that people may not recognize their own negative thought patterns, confrontation can be one of the best tools to help them change. When you reflect back to them what they are thinking and feeling, they can become more self-aware and work to correct their thinking habits.

FOCUSING ON THE VISION

As a leader, you can focus on the outcome of a given project and the positive results you hope to see, as this will help your team members enter more positive thought patterns. If you notice that there is someone who is unwilling to move into a space of higher positivity, you will need to confront them directly or even part ways with them, as their energy can limit new ideas and impede the mission before you.

Positivity can be very rewarding for both you and everyone around you, which is why it's so important to work on generating positive energy every chance you get. Bring that energy any time you have your team together and home in on the vision of the company. It's crucial not only for the company's external image but for the dedication and motivation of each employee.

CHAPTER TEN

PURPOSE

● ● ● ● ● ● ● ●

Purpose is the soul of any project. You can have great skills or a great education, but without purpose, it will be difficult to make your vision come to life. Leaders who have a strong purpose know where they are going and so they can achieve the steps that need to be taken to get there. Without purpose, without a destination, you will simply tread water, stuck in the same place. Purpose gives you a shore to aim for and swim toward.

IKIGAI

Ikigai is a Japanese concept that speaks well to the idea of purpose. The word *ikigai* comes from two parts: *iki* meaning life, and *gai* meaning value. *Ikigai* can be related to a career, but it is just as often connected to hobbies, leisure interests, or time with family and friends. A good example of *ikigai* can be seen in the movie *Jiro Dreams of Sushi*. The movie tells the story of Jiro Ono, who is considered by many to be the best sushi chef in the world. In fact, he owns the restaurant that Barack Obama visited during his trip to Japan. Jiro's restaurant is highly sought after, and you often need to make a reservation months ahead of time. Why? The quality of what he creates is unsurpassed. When Jiro visits the local fish markets, he takes the time to choose the freshest fish and will never settle for anything less. He is highly respected in the markets, as he can recognize freshness very easily. Sushi is Jiro's career, but it is also his *ikigai*. It is what he is passionate about and what makes him feel excited to start each day. Sushi gives his life purpose.

In Western cultures, *ikigai* has been translated into the idea of finding your "dream job." This isn't an incorrect way to think about *ikigai*, but it is a more limited version than the original Japanese concept. *Ikigai* promotes a profound engagement with what you do, both at work and in the rest of your life. The Japanese surround themselves with *ikigai* and use it to guide them in everything they do, while Westerners tend to use the concept in a much more specific way.

GANBATTE

Ganbatte is another Japanese term. It translates in English to "do your best." This is related to the concept of *ikigai*, as when the

Japanese find their *ikigai*, they use *ganbatte* to engage with it. They understand that when you do your job to the best of your ability and combine it with the meaning the job gives you, you are fulfilling your purpose.

Going to work and doing daily tasks can feel robotic, but once you add soul to the machine through purpose, everything comes alive. When leaders have their own purpose, they can inspire and motivate others to do the same. The leader is the soul of an organization and can animate everything else happening around them with the right mindset.

DEFINING YOUR PURPOSE

There are two levels of purpose that I will discuss here. The first is the personal level of purpose. Here, you can look for values to help you define your purpose and create your own *ikigai*. For example, I discovered that my personal purpose is to inspire others, and I based that purpose on the values of family, career, and love. I want to inspire others, help people find new insights, and become better versions of themselves. Using this purpose as my guide, I started doing activities that would help me achieve that. I began to write, speak, and make movies in order to spread inspirational content.

The second level of purpose is the company purpose. This relates to your personal purpose, as you can try to match the two in order to find fulfillment in your work. For example, imagine that someone values sustainability and their purpose in life is to help others live a more sustainable lifestyle. To find work that will feel meaningful to them, they can search for a company that is developing sustainable technologies or whose goal is to offer products aimed at sustainability. A company's purpose can inspire you to pursue your personal purpose.

Not every task at every job will be directly related to your purpose, but your purpose can help you find meaning even in those tasks. For example, when I am making a movie, my goal is to create a film that will inspire others. To prepare the movie, however, I have to search for investors, write the script, find and manage a film crew, edit the movie, and so on. I regularly come across tasks that aren't in my area of interest or expertise, and I must ask for help in those cases. Editing, for example, is a huge task and not something I always enjoy, but when I think of my purpose—making a movie that will inspire others—it gives me clarity on how to edit the movie in a way that will achieve that. In the end, your purpose is what drives you to persevere, even when you encounter difficult or boring moments or tasks.

How to Recognize Purpose in Yourself and Others

A sense of purpose can often be recognized through how focused someone's activities are. If we think of a scale, those who would score 10 would be those who have a clear purpose in life and organize all of their activities around that purpose.

Let's look at Marie Kondo as an example. As a child, she became fascinated with cleaning and tidying up the spaces in her home and school. She would tidy the kitchen in her home, organize her family's clothing, and even throw things away occasionally! As she grew, she cultivated this passion and developed it into her purpose. She now seeks to help people spark joy by organizing and tidying their personal spaces and filling them with things that bring them happiness. Her book *The Life-Changing Magic of Tidying Up* is a *New York Times* bestseller, and she has been able to reach thousands of people through her work in this area. She would easily score a 10 on the purpose scale, as she has identified her purpose and organizes her life around it.

Another example of this is Marshall Goldsmith. His purpose is to help leaders improve, and he has built his career around that purpose. He coaches leaders through how to be better, teaches others how to coach, and also gives presentations and speeches about leadership. That is his focus, and that is where he puts his energy.

The opposite of a purpose-driven person would be someone who is unsure what they're aiming for. They engage in many different activities and change their mind often. Overall, they seem indecisive when it comes to where to focus their energy. Alternatively, those who lack a purpose may do very little, choosing instead to spend their time in front of the TV or scrolling through social media. These are the people who would score very low on the purpose scale.

| 1 | 2 | 3 | 4 | 5 | 6 | 7 | 8 | 9 | 10 |

←————————————————————————————————————→

LOW PURPOSEFULNESS   **HIGH PURPOSEFULNESS**

This is a scale you can use to measure the purposefulness of each member of your team and then discuss what may need to be improved.

●

How to Verbally Communicate Purpose

Purpose can be communicated when you take the time to paint a picture of your vision so that others can imagine it and even decide to be a part of it. Using clear details, you can draw people into how you imagine the future. For example, when I was eighteen, I decided to study law. My main purpose at the time was to pass the university entrance exams and score high enough to get a full scholarship. When speaking with my classmates one day, they asked me what I was planning to study in university, and I told them about my intention to study law. I began to describe how, to me, law was like a book full of magic spells. To read the spells, you must master the language, and only a select few reach that point. They obtain a lot of power because that language can change people's lives. I was so descriptive and imaginative in the way I described my vision that I inspired half of my classmates to also look into studying law. While very few did, the key idea here is that if you have your own strong vision and sense of purpose, you can convey that to others and inspire them to seek their own purpose.

Another powerful way to share vision and purpose with others is to use hypnotic language. Pioneered by the psychiatrist Milton H. Erickson, hypnotic language is designed to bypass conscious resistance by using inference and suggestions to communicate directly with a listener's subconscious mind.

Phrases like *you may find, you could, can you imagine, you probably already know that, sooner or later, how would it feel if you, I do not know if, you might notice* are powerful ways to hypnotically introduce an idea to the subconscious mind without conscious resistance.

Hypnotic language can help a leader encourage their team to internalize their vision because this kind of communication works both on the rational and emotional level. Used with integrity and when aligned with values, it can allow ideas to take hold far more powerfully than direct communication. Of course, there are applications for this technique outside the office too! For example, my children are seven and five years old. Recently they saw me reading and asked about what I was doing. I told them that reading is like watching a movie in your mind, and I used hypnotic language to communicate this idea. Two weeks later, my kids were reading aloud to each other.

Effective hypnotic suggestion leaves space for others to fill in the missing pieces of your artfully vague language, achieving the result of your intention without you even having to state it explicitly enough to invite disagreement or resistance.

CREATING ALIGNMENT WITH PURPOSE

While it's important to share your vision and purpose, make sure you do it with integrity. This means that you recognize the values of the other person and don't try to convince them of something that will go against those. Instead of forcing your purpose on others, you can align your purpose with that of someone else to create even more strength. For example, if my purpose is to inspire others and someone else's purpose is to promote innovation, we can combine our visions and develop ideas that will serve both.

ACTIONS WITHOUT PURPOSE

Imagine meeting a friend who is pursuing a PhD. When you speak to them, they come alive with enthusiasm. They feel inspired by what they are learning and have plans to start a business aligned with what they are studying. They are getting their PhD in order to serve a specific purpose, and you can feel this when you speak to them.

Now, imagine you meet another friend who is also pursuing a PhD. When you ask them about it, they tell you they are just doing it in order to make more money at their current job. They may tell you about a class or two, but they don't seem particularly interested in talking about it. This is a good indication that this action is not purpose driven.

How to Use Your Body Language and Micro Expressions to Be Congruent with Purpose

When thinking about body language and micro expressions that demonstrate a sense of purpose, we can refer back to the chapter on integrity. Remember that integrity is about being congruent with who you are. Purpose is also about being authentic, but it relates more to the "why" of your actions. For that reason, integrity and purpose are closely aligned at the body language level.

THE ENGINE

Purpose is like an engine, and in order for an engine to work smoothly, it needs to be aided by the various elements in the rest of the machine. If you think of your body as that machine, your body language will be aligned with the purpose you are putting forward. When talking about your purpose, your body should become more animated and alive. For example, imagine a man visiting the beach with his family. He is about to fall asleep as his wife and children play in the water. Then he gets a phone call from work, jumps up, and enters an animated conversation. Watching this scene, you can likely conclude that his purpose in life revolves around his work and not around his family.

When speaking about your purpose, your body language should also be congruent with what you are saying. For example, if you tell a friend that you love to inspire people in your work and your body language is open and relaxed, this demonstrates congruence in what you are verbally saying and what your body is demonstrating, which suggests honesty.

If someone tries to say that they care about something that isn't actually related to their purpose, their body language will show signs of hesitation or discomfort, such as scratching their head, raising an eyebrow, or crossing their arms. This can sometimes happen when a company prepares a speech for an employee but the employee doesn't believe what they are saying. They will be resistant to the purpose they are putting forward in the speech.

Review this table to learn more about specific gestures and micro expressions that demonstrate a sense of purpose and which demonstrate a lack of it:

BODY LANGUAGE AND MICRO EXPRESSIONS THAT INDICATE PURPOSE	BODY LANGUAGE AND MICRO EXPRESSIONS THAT SUGGEST A LACK OF PURPOSE
• Eye contact	• Crossed arms
• Smiling/nodding	• Scratching head or eyelid
• Relaxed posture	• Raised eyebrow
• Open hands	• Tapping with fingers
• Hand gestures (enthusiasm)	• Touching nose or mouth

BODY LANGUAGE AND MICRO EXPRESSIONS THAT INDICATE PURPOSE (CONT.)	BODY LANGUAGE AND MICRO EXPRESSIONS THAT SUGGEST A LACK OF PURPOSE (CONT.)
• Symmetrical, happy smile with both lip corners up	• Eyes widened in fear or brows furrowed in anger
• Uneven smile with only one lip corner up (a micro expression of contempt but with the timing that can indicate courage or purpose)	• Nose wrinkled in disgust

How to Recognize Purpose in Body Language and Micro Expressions Using the BLINK Technique

To use the BLINK technique to discover someone's purpose, I suggest starting with two alternate visions to see which one resonates more. For example, you can first present a vision around the purpose of inspiring others: "For some people, it's very important to inspire others, so they choose activities that help trigger change in others, such as speaking, writing, presenting, making movies, or taking photos. These are all ways they can express themselves and inspire those around them."

In this example, notice that there are various activities mentioned, and people will inevitably react more strongly to some of these activities. For example, a person may hate speaking but really enjoy writing and sharing their ideas through books and articles. As you speak, you can notice how their facial expressions change when you mention each activity.

As an alternative, you can present a vision that revolves around making money: "Some people focus more on making money. They love to see calculations that show growth, and they focus on activities that improve profit margins. If marketing, speaking with clients, or coaching team members will increase profits, that is where they will focus their attention."

Again, in this scenario you can see how people react not only to the overall purpose of making money but to the activities that may be associated with that.

WHY IT'S IMPORTANT TO DISCOVER SOMEONE'S PURPOSE

Making a connection between a leader's purpose and the various purposes of the team members is important in any company. If a leader can understand what is driving their team members to come to work and feel motivated, they can integrate that into the goals and vision of the team. If there are competing purposes, you can make that work for everyone, but first you need to know what each person's purpose is, which is where BLINK comes in.

It's important not to put down the purposes of individuals. Even if your purpose is to inspire others, you shouldn't look down on those who are more focused on making money. These are different ways to approach work, but they can both lead to increased motivation when they are embraced. As a leader, you need to gather together the various purposes in your team, create a vision that respects all of them, and use that vision to help people feel respected and heard in their workplace.

Integrating Purpose into Who You Are

Living with purpose can create an engine that will drive your activities forward. If you have a purpose, it can create energy around everything you do and help you feel that you're living a more meaningful life. To discover your purpose, you can look at four different areas, which I cover here.

WHAT ARE YOU PASSIONATE ABOUT?

If you know what you love to do, this can be a great place to start when trying to discover your purpose. I had a friend who finished her degree in psychology with me. At first, she thought she would work with people to counsel them through emotional hardships, but she soon realized that working with people wasn't something she loved to do. Instead, she discovered a love of numbers and eventually became an accountant. This still allowed her to work with people but on a more limited basis that felt better for her. She had to be honest with herself about what she enjoyed doing, even though it was a surprise to her at the time.

WHAT ARE YOU GOOD AT?

It's possible that you are passionate about something that you aren't very good at, and it's important to recognize that. For example, I love to play the saxophone, but I also recognize that I don't play very well. Because of that, it's something I take time to do as a hobby but not as a career playing for the public. Sometimes the simple truth is that what you love and what you're good at aren't the same, and that's okay.

WHAT DOES THE WORLD NEED?

When thinking about your purpose, it's important to consider what the world needs and how you can use what you enjoy and what you're good at to connect to that need. For me, it was about making movies. I first discovered that I had a passion for making movies, and then I realized that I was very good at the editing process, as I had a great memory when it came to the conversations and scenes that had been filmed, which made it easy to put everything together into a cohesive film. People also seek out inspiring movies, so it was something the world needed, and I was able to develop it into my purpose.

HOW CAN YOU BE PAID FOR IT?

Once you've identified the elements, you can reflect on how you can get paid for the thing you've identified as your purpose. For example, maybe you've identified coaching as something you enjoy, something you're good at, and something the world needs.

You can then decide to become a coach, which clients will pay for. Coaching may require other elements, such as budgeting or planning, and if you aren't good at those things, you can always delegate them to someone else. In that way, you can focus on what you really love.

Helping Others Integrate Purpose into Their Lives

Not everyone knows their purpose. An individual may engage in many different activities based on what they are good at without defining any of those activities in relation to a life purpose. When you notice this as a leader, you can use the four questions from the previous section to guide them toward a better understanding of their purpose. When they understand how these four things relate to one another and to their skills, they may be able to focus their attention more and discover their purpose.

If you have team members that do a little bit of everything and aren't sure what to focus on, by creating this understanding about their passions and strengths, you can create activities and tasks that more closely match what they prefer to spend their time on. If you've organized your team well, you will always have people with a variety of skills and can delegate tasks that represent both what they are good at and what they enjoy, which can increase overall motivation within your team.

CORRECTING A MISALIGNMENT

If you notice someone is complaining or focusing on the negative, it may be that their tasks aren't aligned with their purpose, and they don't feel engaged. This can happen when someone first starts working at a company, as their résumé will often reflect many skills, which they've included to increase their chances of getting a job. But that doesn't mean that all tasks related to those skills will be enjoyable for them, which can lead to problems in their motivation if they're given the wrong task. If you notice this, it's a good time to approach the team member to discuss their purpose and goals and help their work align with that in the best way possible.

For example, when I was in primary and secondary schools, I didn't like math. I didn't see a purpose in working with numbers and calculations, and I wasn't particularly good at it. I preferred to write poetry or learn Arabic during my math classes. But when I was working toward my degree in psychology, I had to use numbers to create statistics and develop correlations, and I finally found a purpose for math and began to enjoy it.

This is an important lesson for leaders, as well. If your team members don't understand the purpose behind what they are doing, they won't feel motivated or interested in it. Take the time to help your employees understand their own purpose, as well as the company's purpose. If you can relate all of it to each individual's *ikigai*, they will do their best to fulfill what is asked of them and enjoy it in the process.

CONCLUSION

The Era of the Lone Leader Is Over

A business leader used to be a solitary figure high upon the mountain who led the silent, obedient pack. That era is over. The old model of leadership has given way to a new model that emphasizes the interplay of the leaders and the whole team.

Instead of a lonely, isolated figure, a leader today is more like the conductor of a symphony orchestra. The conductor ensures the whole orchestra is in unison, with every player performing at their best in their own unique way. Creating a company is about creating this beautiful symphony of skills and personalities.

By bringing together the ten leadership qualities we have discussed in this book, we empower our teams with understanding and openness. We communicate with integrity and self-awareness, to bring out the best in those we are called upon to lead. And then, together, we can change the world!

Good leadership is not about imposing your ideas on others; it's about empowering the top professionals who are part of your team and allowing their vision to blend with your vision, creating a beautiful new montage of possibilities.

A good leader is open-minded and provides space for everyone on their team. Sometimes, they may even need to step aside to let others share their ideas and inspirations, and to have their moment to shine.

A good leader is not perfect. It is not possible to achieve perfection, and it is actually better not to be perfect. Leaders are called upon to manage complex organizations populated by even more complex and often contradictory human beings. We began by looking at the *kasuri* pattern, and how the very imperfections and imprecision of this pattern are the key to its beauty.

No great leader embodies all ten of these leadership qualities perfectly at all times. But you can hold them in your mind and strive toward them.

As you think about the qualities and techniques you have learned, you will find yourself more attentive to them in others in both your professional and personal lives. You will notice when someone is communicating to you with integrity (and when someone may not be). You will observe courage in people whom you had previously not given their due. You will realize when someone is approaching you with purpose and the courage of their convictions, and when someone may be hesitant and unsure of themselves.

Like a child absorbing their first language through conversation and osmosis, you will start to develop an ear for the language of leadership and begin to speak it, at first consciously and later automatically. Use these ten qualities to guide your evolution and be the leader, like Marshall Goldsmith, who inspires others and dances, imperfectly but congruently, with the complexities and human potential with which you are charged.

CONCLUSION

The world is not black and white; it is full of shades. When looking at a rainbow, it is almost impossible to focus on any individual color because they all blend and spill into one another. Leadership is the same; it is about allowing the different elements to come together to create something greater than any individual could. The role of the leader is to create space with others and to allow others to shine.

INDEX